# The Laugh shall be first

The Very Rev. Dr James A Simpson

with a Foreword by
ROSAMUNDE PILCHER

To Alison.
with every good wish

SAINT ANDREW PRESS

First published in 1998 by
SAINT ANDREW PRESS
121 George Street, Edinburgh EH2 4YN


Copyright © James A Simpson 1998

ISBN 0 7152 0763 6

**British Library Cataloguing in Publication Data**
A catalogue record for
this book is available
from the British Library

ISBN 0715207636

This book has been set in 10/14 pt Melior.

**Cover design** by Mark Blackadder.
**Cover and text illustrations** by Tim Archbold.
**Printed** and **bound** in Great Britain by Redwood Books, Trowbridge, Wiltshire.

# Contents

# *Dedication*

This book is affectionately dedicated
to my grandchildren
Sally, Rhona, Isla, Liam, Katherine, and Kyle
who all have a great capacity for fun and laughter.

# Foreword

SOME years ago my husband and I bought, as a holiday house, a flat over the Bank of Scotland, in Dornoch. We did this for a number of reasons. It was an area of Scotland that we both knew and enjoyed. My husband is a keen golfer, and I always longed to get back to the sea and to beaches similar to those I had known and loved during my Cornish childhood. Our grandchildren could come and stay; we would lend the flat to impoverished young friends in need of summer vacations. It is also pleasant to have a bolt hole, when day to day life becomes a little wearing and it is time to get away.

All of this took place as we had planned.

But as well, unsuspected bonuses came our way. One of these was the proximity of the flat to the Cathedral, the Parish Church of Dornoch. Our upstairs sitting-room faces out over this ancient building just a street's width away, and whatever the weather, or time of day, it is always a visual joy. Veiled in the leaves of summer trees, it glows in the after-noon sunshine of an August day. When the winds pour in from the North sea, it stands impervious to the gales, and at night the floodlights come on and the tower is caught in theatrical illumination. One Christmas Eve we watched the blown snow swirling and falling, twinkling from white to gold in the darkness. The sight was as magical as a toy snow-storm, caught in a glass bubble.

Sometimes, on summer evenings, the faint strains of music can be heard, the organist having a quiet practice. The soft chords mingle with the cries of kittiwakes and jackdaws.

The other bonus was meeting the minister of the Cathe-dral, Dr James Simpson. We crossed the street and attended morning service whenever we could. It was a real pleasure to worship in a packed congregation in a lovingly preserved and cared for church, and listen to the preaching of Dr Simpson. It became clear to me early on that here was a man, not only devout, learned and humane, but one blessed with an irrepressible sense of humour.

In Ecclesiastes we are told that to everything there is a season – a time to weep and a time to laugh. One of Dr Simpson's stories was about a small child who truly believed that the gifts of the Magi to the newborn Christ were Gold, Frankincense and Mirth.

We had only been in Dornoch for a little while before we were privileged to meet James and his wife Helen on less churchly ground. We shared meals and other convivial get-togethers. These were always characterised by much laughter as he shared with us humorous anecdotes, many of which are included in his little books, *Holy Wit, Laughter Lines* and *All about Christmas* (Gordon Wright Publishing).

As a writer I have always felt that no novel should be either all comedy or tragedy, because everyday life is like a long plait of different coloured yarns, where sadness and joy, tears and laughter, are all twined tightly together. At the most doleful of moments, an unexpected occurrence can turn gloom to mirth. It is a skilful author who navigates between the two extremes of emotion.

One of my favourite novels is *The Pursuit of Love* by Nancy Mitford. Each time I re-read it, I giggle my way through the dotty goings on of the Radleys. Uncle Matthew gnashing his dentures, working himself into the most terrible of rages, and venting his spleen on a flock of innocent Nuns, so certain was he that they were damned German parachutists. And Davey Warbeck, who twisted a tonsil singing 'Where Pants the Hart' at one of the family weddings. And then … turn the last page and the reader finds tears filling his or her eyes. So

neatly, so quickly, all the little strings of the plot are tied up.
So poignant is the outcome that one can scarcely bear the
sadness for all those bright and funny young people.

In the pages of this book, Dr Simpson speaks of the healing qualities of laughter. As well as the soft word, laughter
can dissolve anger. The actor Derek Nimmo told me once of
how his wife was walking down Sloane Street in London,
on a cold winter's day, well wrapped in her mink coat. She
was accosted by a woolly hatted lady, avid for animal rights,
who latched on to Mrs Nimmo's furry lapel and shook it
fiercely, demanding, 'What poor tortured creature died so
that you could wear this coat?' Mrs Nimmo replied, 'My
mother in law.'

So read this thoughtful collection of essays about the
nature and history of laughter. Absorb Dr Simpson's wisdom
and humour. And laugh.

ROSAMUNDE PILCHER

# *Introduction*

THIS book had its beginnings in the William Barclay lecture given each year in honour of Professor William Barclay, one of the most popular writers and broadcasters of the twentieth century. I counted it a great honour in 1997 to be invited to deliver this memorial lecture, for William Barclay had not only been my New Testament professor, he had officiated at my wedding and come out of retirement to baptise my son Graeme. In the college choir which he conducted, he tolerated my limited musical gifts. He encouraged me to write my first book. He taught me more about communicating with ordinary people than anyone else. I doubt if he could have been uninteresting even if he had tried.

Early on in my preparations for the Barclay lecture, which I decided to entitle, '*The Laugh shall be first*', my Calvinistic muscles twitched on several occasions. I could almost feel John Calvin breathing down my neck and saying, 'You ought to use this unique occasion to speak about more weighty matters than laughter'. But the more I thought about it, the more convinced I became that my choice of subject would have had Dr Barclay's approval. Like me, he would have included humour among the cardinal virtues, and humourlessness among the deadly sins.

In an article which he wrote for the *British Weekly*, Dr Barclay told of a little girl who informed her mother that an Indian boy had joined their class. When her mother inquired if he spoke English, she said, 'No, but he laughs in English'. Dr Barclay then continued, 'Laughter is one of the most infectious things in the world. Laughter begets laughter. A good test of a committee or board or a church court is how

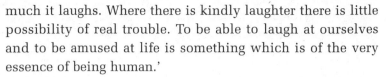

much it laughs. Where there is kindly laughter there is little possibility of real trouble. To be able to laugh at ourselves and to be amused at life is something which is of the very essence of being human.'

Stephen Leacock said earlier this century: 'In a world that studies and teaches everything that can be studied and taught, humour alone remains an unexplored field. What laughter is, and why it is, what is a sense of humour and why you get it, what a joke is and why it is a joke, all these things remain unascertained.' Since these words were penned, laughter has been extensively analysed. The dullness of some of the resulting academic treatises has reinforced my belief that one of the dangers of trying to define humour and laughter is that in the process you are liable to lose your sense of humour.

In this little volume I have tried to do several things – to highlight the importance of cultivating that side of the human spirit that expresses itself in humour and laughter; to reinforce the clearly established link between humour and mental and physical health; and to counteract the mistaken but common belief that seriousness is the hallmark of maturity, and humour an indication of immaturity and triviality. Life is not simply about diligence and duty, vigilance and crusading. It is also about play and relaxation, fun and laughter, about being glad to be alive.

Convinced that laughing is more important than defining or analysing laughter, I have included at the end of each chapter (except the one entitled 'a time not to laugh') short anecdotes and witty remarks which made me laugh, and which I hope will exercise the reader's chuckle muscles.

I gratefully acknowledge my indebtedness to Dr John Peterson, John McKinlay and the Rev. Uist Macdonald for their careful reading of the manuscript. I am grateful also to the Editors of the Irish *Presbyterian Herald* and *Life & Work* for permission to reprint some of the anecdotes from my regular monthly columns.

*The royalties from this book will be used to further research into Cystic Fibrosis. It is my sincere hope that geneticists and doctors working in this field might make it possible for young people like my grand-daughter Sally to enjoy a better quality of life.*

JAMES A SIMPSON

*'Mirth is the medicine of God.'*
RALPH WALDO EMERSON


*'Laughter is the closest thing to the grace of God.'*
KARL BARTH

# The Overlooked Sense

IN his wonderful television series 'Life on Earth', David Attenborough raised the question as to what, if anything, makes us unique or distinctive among the multiple forms of life on earth. He listed things which human beings did which other animals did not do. According to Attenborough, one of these distinctions was sharing a joke. Though animals are capable of happiness, pleasure, games, perhaps even teasing, the sharing of a joke goes beyond the possibilities of other species. It is significant that thousands of years before Attenborough, Aristotle spoke of human beings as 'creatures who laugh'. For the ancients, the day a child uttered its first laugh was a vitally important one. Laughter they believed transformed a human into a human being. I have long wished that, at some stage in their education, people were given a course on the great masters of comedy, for the comic sense is an important part of what it means to be human and humane. It ought to be nurtured, for the ability to see the humour in words and everyday happenings, to delight in ambiguity and nonsense, to be amazed and amused by life, ranks among the most profound and imaginative of human characteristics.

The Bible reminds us how, on the first day of history, 'the morning stars sang together'. An old American Indian legend tells how God having made us so that we were able to talk, run, see and hear, was still not satisfied. So he gave us the gift of laughter. Then God said, 'It is good. Now you are fit to live'. Adversity being present in the world, I wonder if God sought to compensate by giving us a sense of humour, the ability to perceive and appreciate the incongruous in life. I often think of laughter as God's hand on the shoulder of a troubled world, given to us almost as a counterbalance to life's pain and tragedy. Above one of the doors of the Abbey where Sir Walter Scott is buried is the inscription: 'Sweeten bitter things with gentle laughter.' Laughter *does* help us transcend life's heartbreaks and jumbled contradictions. Just because tears sometimes stain our faces, laughter is all the more necessary. In ancient Greece the Greek Comedies offered a counterbalance to the tense emotions elicited by the Greek Tragedies. Whereas in the latter the darkness gradually deepens, in the comedies dark moments are overcome. The last word is with celebration, joy and new life.

David Kossoff has a lovely piece about humour:

*Lord I want to be serious about being funny*
*Humour Lord, the sense of humour,*
*Not included in the senses census*
*(Play on words Lord, ignore it.)*
*The other five are but the servants*
*of the overlooked one!*
*A touch of Heavenly genius Lord.*

Though humour, like intelligence, cannot be precisely defined, I believe God intended it to be enjoyed.

I am told that in the past, when you left a restaurant in the Middle East, the waiter or waitress would say, 'Go smiling'. To this it was customary to reply, 'As God wills it'. I like that. It is a needed reminder that God is on the side of smiles and laughter. Now, I am well aware that a smile can become a smirk, and laughter derisive. 'One may smile and smile and be a villain,' said Shakespeare's Hamlet. Geoffrey Chaucer wrote of a 'smiler with a knife under his cloak'. A smile can also be the expression of cruel satisfaction.

*There was a young lady of Riga*
*Who went for a ride on a tiger*
*They returned from the ride*
*With the lady inside*
*And a smile on the face of the tiger.*

~ Anon ~

On the other hand, few things are more attractive than the smile or laugh of a baby. It is so genuine and without guile. How attractive also is the warm sincere smile of an adult! Such a smile is the lighting system of the face and the heating system of the heart. Mary Angelou counsels women to smile and laugh often. 'It makes you pretty,' she says. Whereas a half-hearted smile scarcely uses the mouth or eyes, the genuine smile grows in a wreath all round the front teeth. Smiling keeps the face from congealing. I cherish the remark of the little girl who was rebuked one day in class for laughing. 'Please Miss,' she said, 'I was just smiling and the smile burst.' For me there are few greater satisfactions than that of making unhappy and sick people smile and laugh again. Like faith, laughter can renew hope in people, and the will to live.

The sound of kindly laughter has always seemed to me the most delightful music in the world. The finest ministers I have known believed that life at its best is a blend of seriousness and humour, sense and nonsense, sacred matters and comic interludes. They all practised a religion that had a deep and joyous laugh in it. Their humour was not something dragged in or glued on. It suffused their whole thinking.

Having written several books of clerical and family humour, it was not surprising that in 1994, when I was nominated Moderator of the General Assembly of the Church of Scotland, one national newspaper carried the heading, 'Church chooses Joker for Moderator'. I assured those who asked that though I would not tell jokes at the Assembly to raise a laugh, nor impose contrived humour on the debates, I would without hesitation use humour if it was spontaneous, if it emerged from the immediacy of what was being said, for kindly humour can enrich business meetings. It can also highlight truth, defuse tension and take the edge off exasperation.

Pope John XXIII, who inspired the sweeping reforms of Vatican II, who cut through centuries of red tape and official procedure, who introduced such a conciliatory and liberating spirit to the papacy when he was elected in his late seventies, had both a caring nature and a wonderful sense of humour. He once said, 'God must have known for 77 years that I would become Pope. Why could he not have made me more photogenic?' Visiting one of Rome's least attractive prisons, the Regina Coeli, he joked with the inmates, 'You could not come to see me, so I have come to see you'. On another occasion he said, 'I often lie half-awake at night and begin to think about a serious problem; I say to myself that I must consult the Pope about it. Then I wake up completely, and remember that I *am* the Pope.' Though considerably overweight and certainly not handsome, the paparazzi loved to photograph him, for he had such a kindly laugh and smile. Louis Michael entitled his book *The Humour and Warmth of Pope John XXIII.* In it he comments on the fact that it was because of the genuine warmth and lively wit of this humble man, that Protestants, long suspicious of Rome, came willingly to his Vatican Council as special guests.

Though the church is not always associated in the minds of people with mirth and humour, some of the wittiest people and finest raconteurs have been those who have had the deepest commitment to what the Church at its finest stands for.

RON Ferguson, the minister of St Magnus Cathedral, tells how while studying in North Carolina, he served as assistant in a local church. Having agreed to lead the early morning Easter service, he was devastated when he awoke at 7 am, an hour after the start of the service. Later that morning, as he read the lesson at the 11 am service, the words of the Easter story acquired a very personal meaning for him. 'He is not here … He is risen.'

The Bishop of Northampton was chairing a meeting at which there were seated at the front several mayors and others, all sporting their gleaming chains of office. The pomp of the meeting was reduced to hilarious uproar when the Bishop began, 'A warm welcome to all – including the chain gang in the front row'.

The Rev. Sabine Baring Gould's grand-daughter told me how it was to accompany a great procession with cross and banners that her grandfather wrote the hymn, *'Onward Christian soldiers, Marching as to war, With the Cross of Jesus, Going on before'*. Unfortunately, at that time controversy raged in the Anglican church over both processions and crosses. Sabine's Bishop, who was strongly opposed to 'graven images', wrote telling him the Cross must not be used in this way. 'What you are permitting verges on the Romish!' When the Bishop next visited, Baring Gould was prepared with a substitute stanza. The choir, without cross, entered singing:

*Onward Christian soldiers,*
*Marching as to war,*
*With the Cross of Jesus*
*Left behind the door …*

The Bishop was not amused.

A minister wrote in his church newsletter: 'No doubt of the remaining 573 members who were not in church on Sunday: some were out of town, some were sick or tending the sick, and many stopped on the way to church to minister to people who had fallen among thieves.'

The distinguished preacher Dr Henry Ward Beecher and Colonel Robert Ingersoll, the vocal atheist, shared a common interest in astronomy. On one occasion, when Colonel Ingersoll visited Dr Beecher's home, he noticed a magnificent working model of the earth, sun and planets. After examining it closely, the Colonel inquired who had made it. 'Who made it?' replied Dr Beecher in simulated astonishment. 'Why nobody made it. It just happened!'

G K Chesterton recalls an encounter with a sceptic who challenged his claim that many intelligent people believed in the Resurrection. When Chesterton listed people like Descartes, Samuel Johnson, Faraday, Gladstone, Pasteur … the young man replied defiantly, 'They had to say that. They were all Christians'. Chesterton's witty comment was

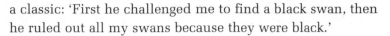

a classic: 'First he challenged me to find a black swan, then he ruled out all my swans because they were black.'

At one of the Trinity College Choir concerts, Dr Barclay told a story about a little girl who was sitting on a wall sucking a large lollipop. She was sticky from ear to ear. When her five year old boyfriend asked if he could have a suck at her lollipop, she said, 'No, but when I am finished and all sticky I will let you kiss me'. Dr Barclay confessed his workload would have been considerably lighter had he been able to say 'no' as politely.

After the Rev. Effie Campbell's daughter married Fergus McCann, the well-known director of Celtic Football Club, Effie was often referred to as Fergus McCann's mother-in-law. She once jokingly said that one of her great dreams was that one day, as she walked through Glasgow in the company of her son-in-law, someone might say, 'Who is *that* with Effie Campbell?'

The Rev. Dr Jones was for many years president of an American theological college. In his youth he had been such a talented golfer that he had thought seriously of becoming a golf professional. Even when he was well into his fifties he was still a scratch golfer. Once during a visit to Pine-hurst he enquired about the possibility of playing the world famous 'Pinehurst No 2' course. When the starter suggested that he might play with a local golfer who was due to tee-off shortly, Dr Jones went and introduced himself to the man who was on the practice ground.

To Dr Jones' surprise the man suggested they play for fifty dollars on the first nine, fifty on the second, and fifty on the game. When Dr Jones said he did not play for money, and certainly *not* for that kind of money, the man said, 'Come on, let's make the round worthwhile'. Slightly upset by his condescending tone, Dr Jones agreed.

Playing better even than usual, Dr Jones won seven of the first nine holes and six of the second nine. In the club-house after the game, having accepted the cheque for $150, he immediately tore it up. 'Let that be a lesson. You never know when your partner might once again be a church minister!'

When he later recounted the incident to friends, one of them said, 'Were you not taking an awful risk? He might also have been a scratch golfer.'

'No,' said Dr Jones, 'there was no risk involved. I saw him hit several shots on the practice ground!'

During his moderatorial year, Dr George Reid visited the Western Isles. The crossing from Harris to North Uist was a horrendous experience, as the small boat was buffeted by gale force winds and mountainous waves. Not only was Dr Reid sea-sick, he actually wondered at one stage if he would ever see dry land again. Shortly after disembarking he was due to preach in Lochmaddy. He began his address by saying that he was tempted to change his text, and preach instead on, 'What came you out to see, a *reed* shaken by the wind?'

Dr Randy Taylor, an American Presbyterian minister and educator, recalled how the mainline denominations in the States took the Gospel out West. 'The Baptists took the word and and walked out West. The circuit rider Methodists rode out West on horseback. The Presbyterians waited for the train.'

After the laughter of his Episcopalian audience had subsided, he added, 'The Episcopalians waited for the Pullman car!'

---

On one occasion a tabloid photographer was having difficulty photographing the former Archbishop of Canterbury, Michael Ramsey. In desperation he finally shouted, 'Archie would you turn your head this way please?'

'My name, sir, is *not* Archie,' the Archbishop replied, smiling warmly, 'It's Mike!'

---

A seminary student, studying to be a priest, decided after two years at seminary to leave to get married. Five years later he and his wife had a child. One day a friend asked him why it had taken them so long. With a twinkle in his eye he replied, 'Well they did not train us for that in seminary!'

---

Keen to sell his car, a minister put an advertisement in a local shop: 'Heavenly body, religiously maintained, host of extras. It could be the answer to all your prayers.'

The words of an old wall plaque – 'If your face wants to smile, let it. If it does not want to smile, make it' – reminded me of how a group of teachers once visited Mother Teresa in Calcutta. When they asked her for some advice to take home to their families, she said, 'Smile at your wives. Smile at your husbands'.

Thinking that this counsel was surprising coming from an unmarried person, one said, 'But you're not married'.

'Yes I am,' she replied with a twinkle in her eye, 'and I find it very hard sometimes to smile at Jesus. He can be *very* demanding.'

Michelle Guiness, the Jewish writer and broadcaster, tells how upset her Jewish mother was when she became a Christian, and later engaged to an Anglican vicar.

Her father's complaint was different. 'If you were going to marry a Gentile, why did you not pick one of the rich members of the Guiness family?'

The Rev. Sydney Smith was one of the great wits of his day. When a landlord angrily said to him, 'If I had a son who was an idiot, I think I would make him a parson,' Smith retorted, without batting an eyelid, 'I see your father was of a different mind'.

Prior to leaving on a Moderatorial visit to Atlanta, a letter arrived inviting me to play Augusta National Golf Course, where the Masters golf tournament is played each Spring. I faxed my acceptance! The day before playing Augusta, I was the guest preacher in the Peachtree Presbyterian Church.

That morning Dr Harrington, the senior minister of the twelve thousand member mega-church, commented on my invitation to play Augusta.

'While Dr Simpson is doing that, I will stay at home here and do the *Master's* work.' He then paused before adding, '... but since I have not been invited, I will pray for rain!'

The following morning I was wakened by the grandfather of all thunder and lightning storms. Turning to my wife I said, 'Whatever Dr Harrington does, he certainly does in a big way!' Fortunately the storm passed and a perfect day ensued.

Dr Angus Stewart tells of a wedding he conducted in the late autumn, The bride arrived at the church 45 minutes late. In announcing the first hymn *'Abide with me'*, Dr Stewart said that although it was not a hymn often sung at weddings, one line did seem especially appropriate in the light of the considerable delay – *'Fast falls the eventide.'*

Archbishop Coggan once said, 'My ignorance of science is such that if anyone mentioned copper nitrate, I should think he was talking about a policeman's overtime'.

The Rev. Blair Monie offered the following preface to a prayer he once gave at a Church meeting. 'Lord I am so happy about how well I have done thus far today. I have not gossiped. I have not been rude. I have not been pushy. I have not been a know-it-all. I really am glad about that. But now I have got to get out of bed …. '

Albert Schweitzer, the distinguished German doctor who was awarded the Nobel Peace Prize for his work in West Africa, was one of my boyhood heroes. While travelling by train from New York to Chicago en route for the Goethe Festival in 1949, a woman who was passing along the corridor noticed his distinguished head of grey hair and big moustache.

Opening the door of the compartment, she asked, 'Do I have the honour of speaking to Albert Einstein?'

Schweitzer smiled and replied, 'No Madame. Though our heads look very much alike on the outside they are very different on the inside'.

To minimise her embarrassment and obvious disappointment, he wrote on a slip of paper, 'Albert Einstein, by his friend Albert Schweitzer'.

# Health and Humour

AN old naval prayer reminds us how laughter, by freeing us from over-seriousness and self-centredness, can allow inner healing to take place. 'Eternal God, give us a keen sense of honour that we may be specially just to those we find it hard to like, and a keen sense of humour that the healing power of laughter may relax life's tensions.'

As far back as Biblical times, a wise man observed that 'a merry heart doeth good like a medicine'. There is not a fibre of our bodies which is not affected by our mental outlook. A scientific study by Lorn Whittaker (in his book *Laugh Away Your Tensions*) discovered that cheerful people resisted disease better than chronic grumblers. He jokingly summed up the scientific evidence by altering the proverb 'the early bird catches the worm' to read 'the surly bird catches the germ'. The film 'Mary Poppins' dramatised laughter's metaphoric lifting power. Though in real life we cannot laugh off gravity, we can laugh off *gravitas,* which literally means over-seriousness. Laughter can ease the weight of life's problems. Laughter and humour relax muscles and relieve stress. They serve as shock absorbers, easing the bumps of life. A person without a sense of humour is like a wagon without springs, jolted by every bump on the road.

Laughing is rather like jogging in the inside. It is good therapy for the lungs. I am told it also stimulates the circulatory system. A Prussian professor, Gottlieb Hufeland, wrote in the nineteenth century:

*Laughter is one of the most important helps to digestion with which we are acquainted. The custom in vogue among our ancestors of aiding the digestive system by having jesters and buffoons present, was founded on valid medical principles. Cheerful and enjoyable companions are invaluable at the dinner table. The nourishment which is received amid mirth and jollity produces light and healthy blood.*

Ulcers cannot grow while we are laughing. I remember once spending a delightful few hours in the company of Harry Secombe. When he laughs – and he laughs often – it is as though his whole anatomy is getting a massage.

Modern medicine has long known that negative emotions can precipitate or exacerbate illness, but recently physicians and psychiatrists have begun to explore and appreciate the other side of that coin – what Aristotle hinted at two thousand years ago when he described the habit of laughter as a bodily exercise precious to health. One psychiatrist is quoted as saying that he has had to treat very few people who were able to laugh at themselves. A hearty sustained laugh is one of the most positive, and cheapest anxiety-reducing experiences. It is a tranquilliser with no side effects.

Jeanne Calmont, the world's oldest woman who died recently at the age of 122, attributed her longevity to 'olive oil, port and laughter'. One is tempted to say, 'she who laughs lasts!' Current research has certainly confirmed that laughter not only expands the lungs, literally letting fresh air into our bodies, it also releases energy-giving hormones and pain-relieving endorphins. Medicine men, in some of the American Indian tribes, would sometimes perform funny stunts to make the sick laugh.

Norman Cousins, former editor of the American magazine *The Saturday Review,* tells how he was admitted to hospital with a serious and painful degenerative disease of the spine, one that could well have proved fatal. When informed that the prognosis was not good, he decided if he was going to die he would spend his last days watching humorous videos and films. He later told how he believed this was a contributory factor in the remission of his illness. In his book *Anatomy of an Illness,* he says, 'I made the joyous discovery that ten minutes of genuine belly laughter had an anaesthetic effect. It gave me at least two hours pain-free sleep'. A hospital in West Birmingham now has what is called a 'laughter therapy clinic'. Those suffering from stress-related illnesses are taught to use laughter to relax. They are asked to recall humorous incidents. Tapes of infectious laughter are also played. I am glad laughter is beginning to take its place alongside other therapeutic measures.

Humour is no laughing matter to the brain. It is a type of release valve that enables us to think the unthinkable and accept the unacceptable. The psychiatrist Victor Frankl, who died in September 1997, lost his wife and children in Hitler's gas ovens. Writing of his experiences in that concentration camp, he told how suicidal despair was the greatest enemy. Living starved and naked in that desperate situation of human folly and sin, he found humour to be one of the soul's best survival weapons, truly a godsend. Those who had a sense of humour fared better in the camp than those who lacked it. Writing later of these appalling years, he says …

*Humour more than anything else in the human make-up, can … rise above any situation, even if only for a few seconds. I trained a friend who worked next to me on the camp building site to develop a sense of humour.*

*I suggested that we invent at least one amusing story daily, about some incident that could happen after our liberation. He was a surgeon and had been an assistant on the staff of a large hospital. So I once tried to get him to smile by describing how he would be unable to lose the habits of camp life when he returned to his former work.*

*On the prison building site (especially when the supervisor made his tour of inspection) the foreman encouraged us to work faster by shouting: 'Action! Action!'*

*I told my friend, 'One day you will be back in the operating room, performing a big abdominal operation. Suddenly an orderly will rush in announcing the arrival of the senior surgeon by shouting, "Action! Action!"'*

There are situations in which it is not easy to sustain our sense of humour, but what a bonus if we can. Sigmund Freud, for example, used the phrase 'gallows humour' to describe the humour of Jews, Serbs and Croats in the Austro-Hungarian Empire. Few Christians have had a livelier sense of humour than the Rev. Sydney Smith. It surfaced even in his last months of sickness and considerable pain. When a friend one day said, 'I hope you are taking proper care of yourself', Sydney Smith replied with a twinkle in his eye, 'Yes I am. My caring consists of eating nothing I like, and doing nothing that I wish!'

The dual tragedies in Mark Twain's life – bankruptcy in 1894 and the death of his favourite daughter Susy two years later – were intensified by the loss for a time of his sense of humour. He moved towards a much darker vision of the world. Unlike Victor Frankl, Twain's life and writings succumbed to that darkness:

*A myriad of men are born. They labour, sweat and struggle for bread; they squabble and scold and fight; they scramble for little mean advantages over one another. Age creeps on. Infirmities follow. Those they love are taken from them until at length ambition is dead, longing for release is in their place. It comes at last, the only unpoisoned gift earth ever had for them, and they vanish from a world where they were of no consequence.*

Mark Twain not only sank further and further into bitterness and rage, but became increasingly suspicious of his staff. Fortunately the writing of his autobiography, begun in 1906, helped rekindle and refocus his sense of humour. He re-discovered the truth of what he had previously written about one of his characters: 'He laughed joyously, loud and often … it cut down the doctor's bills.'

Humour is an important part of any survival kit. Humanity cannot live by seriousness alone. Where there is humour all is not dark. I love the story of the Clydebank lady who was extracted from the rubble of her house during the 1940 blitz. When asked by her rescuers where her husband was, she brushed down her clothes before answering, 'The coward is away fighting in North Africa'.

The Danish philosopher Kierkegaard not only poked fun at the moral incongruities in the church of his day, and the solemn self-importance of some of the clergy, he also poked fun at himself. Once at a party, when he fell on the floor with a stroke which was partially to paralyse him, he said to his friends as they peered anxiously over him, 'Oh let it lie, the maid will sweep it up in the morning'. That may seem fairly grotesque humour. What saved it from being so was his faith in a divine love from which he believed nothing could separate him.

Jewish humour is a remarkable phenomenon. In the midst of a very turbulent and tragic history, the Jews developed a genius for comedy. Jewish humour, like hospital humour, expresses a certain heroic defiance in the face of life's most crushing defeats, an unconquerable nobility of spirit that refuses to permit an oppressor or a prejudiced society to have the last word. Throughout history, the Jews believed that God, in his mercy, gave them humour to stop them becoming bitter, and to protect their optimism. Humour helped them cope with situations and problems they could not change. The original meaning of the Jewish name Isaac was 'he who will laugh'. The Old Testament character of that name knew all about the slings and arrows of outrageous fortune. He was almost killed by his father in childhood. In later life he not only became blind, but was conned by his younger son into bestowing upon him his most precious possession. Isaac's ability to go on laughing in the face of such suffering and humiliation is an early example of humour triumphing over despair. Early this century, when Jews in America were being prevented from joining country clubs, Groucho Marx, on being turned down for membership of a certain swimming pool, asked: 'My son is only half-Jewish. Could he join and go in up to his waist?' If more Orthodox Jews today had such a sense of humour, Jerusalem would be a happier place.

Whereas a hearty laugh is a sign of sanity, lack of laughter is one of the commonest characteristics of insanity. In the book *One Flew over the Cuckoo's Nest,* Rendall Patrick McMurphy writes of the insane asylum he visited: 'The first thing that got me about this place is that there was not anyone laughing. I have not heard a real laugh since I came through that door. Man when you lose your laugh you lose your footing.'

The pianist and comedian Victor Borge claims laughter is the 'shortest distance between two people'. It is also, I believe, the shortest distance between two conflicting points of view. In the dark days of the American Civil War, Abraham Lincoln used to open Cabinet meetings by reading from the writings of the American humorist, Artemus Ward. He did this to settle the nerves of some of the members of the Cabinet, and minimise the risk of them blaming each other when things went wrong. Lincoln said on one occasion, 'With the fearful strain that is on me night and day, if I did not laugh, I should die'.

Kindly laughter oils the wheels of interpersonal relations. It is one of the best solvents for the grit of irritation which constantly gets into the cogs of life. It is like the oil in our car, not exactly one of the working parts, but an ingredient without which the working parts are liable to fail. Kindly laughter is good, refreshing, disarming, cleansing. It can make all the difference between contentment and confrontation. A friend who one day heard Voltaire speak highly of one of his contemporaries, said, 'It is good of you to say such pleasant things of him when he says such unpleasant things about you'. Whereupon Voltaire suggested, 'Perhaps we are both mistaken'.

I would certainly not claim that laughter is the answer to every medical problem. It can occasionally exacerbate problems. A man whose ribs had been broken in a car accident, said to me when I visited him in hospital, 'Please Dr Simpson, don't make me laugh'. There is a time to laugh, and as we shall see in a later chapter, a time not to laugh.

LAUGHTER is the sensation of feeling good all over and showing it principally in one place.

A plumber once did an installation job for a teacher. After two months, when no pay was forthcoming, the plumber phoned the teacher. 'Look, you don't have to pay the whole bill at once, but at least pay part of it.'

When the teacher explained that he was waiting to see if he had done a good job, one that would last, the plumber, instead of reacting angrily, said, 'I bet you are glad teachers are not paid on that basis'.

There was a burst of laughter at the other end of the phone. The next day the bill was paid in full.

During the Second World War an elderly Clydebank couple got out of bed quickly when they heard the air-raid sirens. The man pulled on his trousers and shirt. Hearing the German planes and the explosion of bombs, he rushed with his wife across the open piece of ground behind their home to the communal air raid shelter. As they hurried, his wife accidentally stood on his braces which were dangling behind him. As he made to go forward the elastic stretched. When her restraining foot was removed, the braces shot up and hit him on the back. Turning to her he said in a pathetic voice, 'Oh Jean, you go on. They've got me'.

A ten year old girl had had a really bad day. She had been scolded several times by her parents. That night at dinner, when her father asked her to say grace, she prayed, 'Thou preparest a table before me in the presence of mine enemies'.

Tom Skillen told on the radio how, as a boy, he used to help in his father's shoe-repair shop. One afternoon a little lady brought in her husband's boots for repair. Early the following morning she rushed into the shop. 'Have you started the repair yet?' she gasped. When his father answered that he had not, she said, 'Thank goodness – only do the right boot. My husband was involved in an accident last night and they may have to amputate his left foot'.

It was such an incongruous request that Tom had difficulty restraining his laugh.

Predestination is the idea that compelled one man who fell down a flight of stairs to pick himself up, dust himself off and exclaim, 'I am glad *that's* over with'.

Patrick Mahoney tells what he claims is a true story about a cardinal who was noted for his seriousness. When he lay dying, his relatives, seeing his helplessness, began sharing out his belongings. He lay there watching them, too weak to object. Then he noticed his pet monkey pick up his cardinal's hat, put it on his head, and admire himself in the mirror. At this the old man burst out laughing, and laughed himself back to health.

When Spike Milligan was asked where he was from, he replied 'London'. When asked next, 'Which part?', he replied, 'All of me'.

Spike's colleague, Harry Secombe, once interviewed me for the 'Highway' TV programme. Before the interview, I

commented on his signet ring. He told me he had chosen as his own personal motto 'Go on'.

'You can read it as *Goon*, if you like,' he said.

The blind pianist George Shearing was once travelling by plane. There was to be a scheduled stop at Detroit to let some passengers off and others embark. When the pilot learned that a technical fault would mean a delay of over an hour, he informed the passengers that they were free to disembark if they felt so inclined. Everyone did, except George Shearing. He stayed on board with his guide dog. When the pilot later came through the plane, he noticed George sitting alone. He suggested that if he wanted to stretch his legs, he would accompany him on to the tarmac. George said he was quite happy to stay on board, but if the pilot was willing to take his dog out for a few moments, he would appreciate that. The pilot, who was a dog-lover, agreed. Imagine the consternation on the faces of the returning passengers when they saw the pilot approach the plane with the guide dog!

An army chaplain tells how he was once asked to write a letter, on behalf of a wounded soldier to his wife. When the chaplain asked how he wanted to begin the letter to Mary, the soldier was of little help.

'What about beginning with "Mary my darling wife"?' suggested the chaplain.

'Aye,' he said, 'you put that down Padre. That'll give her a right good laugh to start with.'

A man who sent a joke to the *Reader's Digest* added this postscript: 'If it is not good enough, don't bother sending me a dejection slip.'

# A Funny Way of Being serious

IN an article for *Time Magazine*, T S Eliot reviewed James Thurber's work as cartoonist and author. He wrote, 'Unlike so much humour, Thurber's is not merely a criticism of superficial aspects of society, but something more profound'. Thurber believed that anything that is serious was worthy of humorous comment. He thought in fun, but felt in earnest. Most cartoonists love to highlight the absurdities of political and ecclesiastical life. One portrayed a psychiatrist saying to a prominent politician lying on his couch, 'I can't help you if you're going to answer "No comment" to all my questions'. Another depicted an army chaplain at the bar downing pint after pint with the new recruits. An older soldier sitting in the corner says to his friend, 'There's that unholier than thou outlook'.

Cartoonists, columnists and comedians who poke fun at the idiosyncrasies, hypocrisies and infighting of religious, political and military life, are necessary for a healthy, open society. They recognise that no human institution is other than imperfect. By exposing hypocrisies, vanities, deceptions and outworn customs, humour contributes to human betterment. The best humour is often a funny way of being serious. It is a moral banana skin dedicated to the discomfiture of those who have an over-inflated opinion of themselves. It can cut the pompous strutter down to size. There are shirts that need unstuffing; swollen egos that need to be reminded that no matter how high a throne we think we occupy, we all sit on our bottom. Should snobbery, bigotry, pretentiousness and phoneyness ever die, cartoonists will have a major problem.

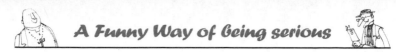

Humour is the court jester in the castle of our soul, protecting us from too solemn or inflated a view of our own importance. It can lead us to say, 'God be merciful to me a fool'.

From mediaeval times the court jester was a common figure in royal circles in Britain. I am told ancient Chinese Emperors and Egyptian Pharaohs employed them, and that in ancient Rome there was a 'fool' market, as well as a slave market. The jester who poked fun at the constant flattery and elaborate protocol of the royal court walked a tight-rope between hilarity and headlessness. Richard Tarleton, Elizabeth I's court jester, was far more honest and candid about the Queen's faults than her chaplains. Scogan, one of Edward IV's court jesters, so annoyed Edward on one occasion with one of his pranks that he was banished and forbidden upon pain of death ever to set foot again on English soil. He duly set out for France, but was soon back in England and in the royal court. When charged with disobeying the king's express prohibition never again to set foot on English soil, he took off his shoes and pointed out that they were full of French soil! Amidst great mirth, he was pardoned and reinstated.

In totalitarian states, humorists have often been the first to go underground. As recently as 1989, the editor of an underground magazine in Czechoslovakia was sentenced to two years in prison for incitement against the state. He had dared crack jokes about the government.

Lin Yutang the Chinese philosopher, writing in 1937, asked, 'Where are the smiles of the European dictators .... Must they look either frightened or dignified or angry, or in any case frightfully serious, in order to keep themselves in the saddle?'

A journalist who interviewed Mussolini tells how, when the typescript was later submitted to be passed for publication, the words 'he laughed' were crossed out.

Social mountaineers who have a career to cut and an impression to make, and people who won't be their age or do their job because they think they are younger or abler than they are, often find it difficult to cope with any situation which does not portray them in a favourable light. Because laughter is perceived as a threat to their reputation or high office, it can evoke violent protests.

Insecure and immature people enjoy laughter directed at others, but not at themselves. For the child and the childish, such laughter can be agony. The capacity to laugh at oneself is a mark of inner security and maturity. Though acquiring that ability can be painful, it is what a mother does when her child makes a clumsy fall. She helps her little one laugh. One may see a child laughing through his tears as he realises his fall is really funny, like a clown's. There is much homely truth in the saying of the old preacher, 'If you could just sit on the wall and see yourself pass by, you would die laughing at the sight'. So long as we permit others to poke fun at our eccentricities, vanities, shortcomings and rituals, there is hope for us and the things we hold dear. I wish more rulers, politicians and ecclesiastics shared the honesty and humility of the spry old lady who was struggling with a small, but obviously heavy case. To a hotel porter who offered to carry it, she said, 'You know you are really getting old when your vanity case outweighs your suitcase'.

While visiting the Riverside Church and Grant's Tomb on the banks of the Hudson River in New York, I heard how General Grant, while on his way to a reception being held in his honour, was caught in a heavy shower of rain. He offered the shelter of his umbrella to a stranger walking in the same direction. The man told Grant that, having never seen the General, he was going only to satisfy a personal curiosity. 'Between you and me,' he said, 'I have always thought him a much over-rated man.'

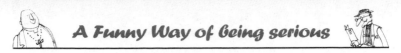

'That is my view also,' said Grant.

Nothing puts people more at ease than self-deprecating humour. I recall a plain-looking man telling how, the first time he played hide and seek, nobody came looking for him. And, speaking at a conference on Humour and Psycho-analysis, John Cleese, of 'Fawlty Towers' fame, introduced himself as Britain's best-known psychiatric patient.

How often in tense situations a witty remark has calmed things down. We rightly speak of 'a saving sense of humour'. It can be disarming. It can turn spears into fishing rods! One evening a crowded train in London screeched to a halt. The passengers were thrown in every direction. Shins were bruised, elbows went into ribs and faces. Tempers were frayed until suddenly a voice was heard to say, 'Unscheduled stop. All change for good nature'.

For years Argentina and Chile, who share a common border, were at war. When peace finally came it was decided to build a statue of Jesus on a prominent site on the border. It was to be made from bullets which had been melted down. The statue came to be known as Christ of the Andes. It was to serve as a reminder how Jesus had said, 'Blessed are the peace-makers'. But alas, when the people of Chile saw that this towering Christ had been built facing Argentina, with his back to Chile, they took it as a deliberate insult. They were so upset that war almost broke out again. But fortunately a wise newspaper editor in Chile pointed out that the positioning of the statue was in fact a great compliment to the people of Chile. Christ, he said, had been depicted gazing down on Argentina because it was Argentina, not Chile, that needed watching! The editor's sense of humour prevented further strife and bloodshed.

The true humorist is never a shallow frivolous person, giggling away. His cap and bells often achieve more in the way of reform than open condemnation. They have often been the means of capturing an audience before getting down to the serious business of crusading for some cause that is dear to his heart. Shakespeare makes King John refer to 'that idiot laughter … a passion hateful to my purpose'. Pompous pillars of the establishment often find it easier to cope with the artillery of fierce criticism than the light infantry of humour. Martin Luther fiercely criticised the veneration of relics in the church of his day – a tooth of John the Baptist, a strand of Christ's beard, a crumb of bread from the Last Supper, a twig from Moses' burning bush. But the criticism for which Luther is remembered is his jest about how the Archbishop of Mainz, not to be outdone by all this, claimed to have two feathers and an egg from the Holy Ghost!

Robert Burns also used mild irony to expose the hypocrisy of the 'Unco Guid' and the 'Holy Willies' of his day. His poetry was characterised not only by the harp, but the scalpel. Burns deserves to be remembered as one of Scotland's great religious reformers. Just as John Knox freed the church of his day from the corruption and autocracy of the mediaeval Roman Church, so Burns, two hundred years later, helped free the Kirk from a deadly pietism and spiritual conceit. The more liberal eighteenth century ministers welcomed his support in their struggle against the extreme Calvinists.

> *O ye, wha are sae guid yoursel,*
> *Sae pious and sae holy,*
> *Ye've nought to do but mark and tell*
> *Your neebours' fauts and folly!*
> *~ Address to the Unco Guid ~*

> *O Thou that in the Heavens does dwell,*
> *Wha, as it pleases best Thysel,*
> *Sends ane to Heaven, and ten to Hell,*
> *A' for Thy glory,*

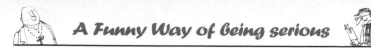

*And no for ony guid or ill*
*They've done before Thee!*

*I bless and praise Thy matchless might,*
*When thousands Thou hast left in night,*
*That I am here before Thy sight*
*For gifts an grace*
*A burning and a shining light*
*To a' this place.*

~ Holy Willie's Prayer ~

In another of his poems, 'Holy Fair', Burns highlights the bizarre double standards of the church:

*Some are fou o' love divine,*
*Some are fou o' brandy.*

Through the satirical mirthquake of such poems, the still small reforming voice was heard in Scotland.

In Denmark Soren Kierkegaard often used satire to try to reform the deplorable state of Christianity in the Established Church of his day. In one meditation he likened the worshippers to geese who, on Sundays, gather for worship. The gander, who preaches regularly, reminds them of their lofty destiny, the high goal the Creator has for them – the goal for which purpose their wings had been designed. At the mention of the word 'Creator', the geese curtsy and the ganders solemnly bow their heads. But as soon as the service is over, they immediately forget all about using their wings to soar to loftier heights. They waddle home and quickly become engrossed in more mundane matters. They not only become plumper, but start ridiculing the few in their midst who are genuinely concerned about the possibility of flying.

Had John Bossidy, in an after dinner speech, simply criticised the aristocratic families of Boston – the Cabots and

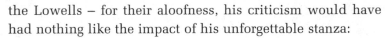

the Lowells – for their aloofness, his criticism would have had nothing like the impact of his unforgettable stanza:

> *And this is good old Boston*
> *The home of the bean and the cod,*
> *Where the Lowells speak only to the Cabots*
> *And the Cabots speak only to God.*

Whereas many comedians are simply resigned to the follies of the human race, and feel the only thing possible is to make a joke of them, the satirist is basically an optimist. The satirist hopes his or her words will not only expose human follies, but might do something to amend them.

In the late 1950s there was considerable discussion in the United States about Alaska joining the Union. At the same time in Arkansas, white schools were refusing to accept black children. When Jack Parr, the American comedian, in one of his nationwide television shows, was asked by his partner, 'Where are we going to get the extra star for the flag if we admit Alaska?', he replied, 'We could always take it from Arkansas'. That half humorous, half serious remark gave many people in Arkansas food for thought, the implication being that a state cannot have the honour of statehood without accepting the responsibility of statehood. George Orwell called such political jokes 'tiny revolutions'.

Just as the tongue probes and touches the exposed nerve of unhealthy hollow teeth, so a witty tongue can expose the shortcomings of hollow people, institutions and practices. It can be a kind of resistance movement, a disturber of the status quo, a lampooner of false dignity and piety, the enemy of the trite. It offers no latitude to platitude. Shakespeare's Falstaff was not simply a fat knight who drank too much. Nobody else in *Henry IV* is as clear-sighted, or speaks his mind so powerfully. While Falstaff enjoyed playing the fool,

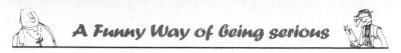

he was in fact an acute observer of people and situations.

Cervantes used humour to wean people away from the unedifying romantic stories about chivalrous knights and fairy princesses. By means of his classic story about Don Quixote, a knight from La Mancha, and his down to earth companion Sancho Panza, who tolerates Don's heroic delusions, Cervantes succeeded in laughing such literature out of existence. He brought Spaniards to their senses with a laugh. The magazine *Punch,* when it started in the 1840s, used the weapon of mild irony to expose social injustice. It was similar with Charles Dickens, who sought to bring into focus an ailing society. Writing in 1840, Thackeray said of Dickens' *Pickwick Papers*, 'We would be wrong to dismiss it as a frivolous work. Dickens' comic masterpiece contains food for serious thought and reflection. Despite a facetious surface, the novel reveals some of the wrongs and beliefs Dickens most wished to attack at the beginning of his career.'

In the film 'The Great Dictator', which Charlie Chaplin wrote and directed in 1940, he used laughter and a series of exaggerated gestures to expose Adolf Hitler for the monster he was. He himself played two roles in the film – the dictator Adnoid Hynkel, and the poor Jewish barber who bore a striking physical similarity to Hynkel. By distorting Hitler's image into a grotesque caricature, Chaplin radically altered his American audiences' perceptions of the goose step and Seig Heil. Nazis were seen for what they were – scary jerks.

The Nobel Prize judges, who in 1997 awarded to the Italian Dario Fo the literature prize, likened him to the 'jesters of the Middle Ages' who relied on wit to poke fun at authority, 'while upholding the dignity of the down-trodden'. The Academy said: 'With a blend of laughter and gravity he opened our eyes to abuses and injustices.' In a piece that Dario Fo wrote for the *New York Times* in 1993 he attacked, with mild irony, corruption in Italian government circles:

'We are a civilised and generous people. All you have to do is look at how we maintain our public servants!' His best known play, 'Accidental Death of an Anarchist', was based on a real event in 1969. A young anarchist, who was under interrogation by the police for a bombing in Milan, fell four storeys to his death in what the police officially called an accident. Others called it murder. The play takes the plot from there, creating a fictional Hamlet-like character known as the fool, who sharply attacks authority, exposing the lies and hypocrisy of officialdom. At one point in the play, when someone questions a statement on a police report, he is told, 'You have a first draft. There have been rewrites'.

G K Chesterton poked kindly fun at many institutions and practices. There being no malice about him, he brought about reforms without making enemies. He produced absurd analogies to drive home his point. He burlesqued many an argument by carrying it one step further. So also did Art Buchwald in the United States. In his book *You can fool all the People all the Time,* he has a delightful piece about a televangelist, the Right Rev. Rolls Royce, preaching about God, sin and the American election. He informs his television audience that they can find out what the Bible has to say about the State and religion, and electing 'the greatest President on this good green globe ... by sending fifty dollars' for a 'velvet-bound illustrated edition' he has had printed. For another hundred dollars, they can have an American flag, one that he has 'personally blessed'. Before the broadcast ends, he tells them to go to their phones and call a toll-free number. 'If God did not want you to have this flag, he would not have let me accept your American Express, Master or Visa cards.'

Advertisers are also well aware how humour can often grab someone's attention. An antique shop sign read: 'Nothing new here'. It can also help implant a brand name. Burma Shave, who used to space out the words of their adverts along American highways, used humour to the full: 'He had the

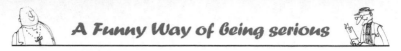

ring – he had the flat – But she felt his chin – and that was that.'

Or 'School ahead – Take it slow – Let the little shavers grow'.

A MAN who travelled regularly by plane was only half-listening to the air stewardess reciting safety instructions. But suddenly his ears pricked up as she said, 'There may be fifty ways to leave your lover, but there are only five ways to leave this plane'. And then, 'Please return your seat to its upright and most uncomfortable position. Later you may lean back and break the knees of the passenger behind'.

A mediaeval legend tells of a man called Marcolf who was reputed to be even cleverer than King Solomon. Marcolf demonstrated time and time again the larger wisdom of the fool. The final straw for Solomon was when Marcolf questioned the wisdom of Solomon having seven hundred wives and three hundred concubines. While Solomon might have been willing to give a little on his wisdom, he was not willing to give on his women! Marcolf was arrested, tried and sentenced to be hanged. On hearing the judgment Marcolf asked if he might be granted one dying request, 'Can I choose the tree from which I will be hanged?'

To Solomon this sounded fair enough. His wish was granted. The legend then concludes, 'Marcolf and the king's soldiers travelled through Jerusalem, and through the valley of Jossafat, and over the hill of Olivet … and through all Arabia, and over the desert to the Red Sea, and *never* did Marcolf find the tree from which he chose to be hanged'.

In a witty postscript to a well known fairy-tale, Garrison Keillor questions whether Cinderella did in fact live happily after marrying the prince. Supervising a large household staff in the palace was hard work. Cinderella often found herself longing for 'the good old days' when she swept the hearth. Finding the constant fawning and flattery in the palace almost unbearable, she and her step-mother met regularly. They often reminisced about their previous minor disagreements. Whereas other people treated her like royalty, her step-mother treated her as a real person. 'My husband won't let me touch a broom, but I go to her house and she puts me to work. I love it. I tell her, 'Mother, you are the only one who yells at me. Don't ever stop. Anger is real. It's honest.'

A quick witted husband, on being accused by his wife of forgetting her birthday, replied, 'How do you expect me to remember, when you never look a day older?'

Several years ago, Hutchesons Grammar Rugby Club and St Aloysius Rugby Club joined to form a united Club. In Glasgow, a city in which religious bigotry still exists, it was a courageous union, Hutchesons being a fine Protestant school and St Aloysius a well known Roman Catholic school. All went remarkably well until the night they had to decide what strip the Hutchesons-Aloysius team would wear. Tension was mounting until one man rose and said, 'Why don't we use the "Hutchie strip" and put Roman numerals on the back!' The laughter which ensued eased the tension.

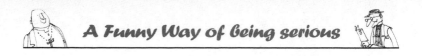

A train conductor announced over the tannoy, 'I have bad news and good news. The bad news is that the engine has broken down; the good news is we are on a train and not a plane'.

When the Jewish philosopher Martin Buber was asked why the Christian world took him more seriously than the Jewish world, he replied, 'Jews are smarter!'

*The Herald* reported how, when a Glaswegian received an envelope with a picture of his car taken by a speed camera, and a note of the fine due, he wrote out a cheque for the amount, photographed it, and sent the photograph to the appropriate address. Back came a repeat demand note with a picture of handcuffs! The welcome humour of this correspondence reminded me how once on the back of a police car there was a notice which read, 'Smile, I could be behind you'.

Shortly after being appointed a Professor in Glasgow University, Dr Murdo Ewen Macdonald was approached to be the senior minister at the City Temple Church in London, renowned for such great preachers as Dr Joseph Parker and Dr Leslie Weatherhead. Dr Macdonald tells how, in the course of the interview, a tweedy lady with an imperious top-drawer public school accent, eyed him severely and barked,

'Professor Macdonald, if you accept our unanimous call, are you prepared to modify your strong Western Isles accent?'

He smiled at her and said, 'On one condition, that you are prepared to modify *your* accent'. Good naturedly she joined in the laughter that followed.

When Steve Abraham paid his considerable tax bill, having used a red pen to complete the pay-in slip, he appended a note, 'This is not red ink. It is blood'. Two days later he received a letter from the tax collector. Clipped to the compliments slip was a sticking plaster.

In the late 1950s, when racial tensions were strong in America, George Thomas, the former speaker of the House of Commons, was invited to preach during a visit to the States. That day he chose as his text, 'In Christ there is no such thing as Jew and Greek, slave and freeman, male and female ...'.

At the end of the service a white man said to him, 'I see you are another one-worlder'.

'That's right,' said George with a smile. 'How many worlds do *you* believe in?'

A dress shop received the following note:

'Dear Madam,
You have not yet delivered the maternity dress I ordered.
Please cancel the order. My delivery was faster than yours!'

A small town Priest, who objected to funeral orations, stipulated in his will that none should be preached at his funeral service. 'It is bad enough to have one priest lying in his coffin, without another lying in the pulpit.'

# A Time not to laugh

LAUGHTER is the mind's intonation, a reliable indicator of character. One can often tell more about a person from the way that person laughs and the things he or she laughs at, than from almost any other kind of mannerism. The epitaph for Billy the Kid – 'He ate and laughed, drank and laughed, rode and laughed, talked and laughed, fought and laughed, killed and laughed' – reveals a great deal about this notorious character. I personally do not find racially-motivated jokes, or jokes about masochism, sadism, addiction and marital unfaithfulness funny, for in real life these things are not funny. They cause a great deal of pain.

I sometimes wonder if there is any level below which humour will not sink. A few years ago a Seattle-based company produced what they called 'The Virgin Mary Immaculate Conception Condoms'. The packet carried a picture of Mary and the baby Jesus. On it was the slogan, 'If you conceive, it is a miracle'. Inside the packet was another picture, this time of Jesus on the Cross wearing a condom. Such sick humour tells me a great deal about the directors of the company. For the sake of notoriety, or a few bucks, or raising a giggle, they are prepared to cheapen and vandalise things others hold sacred. Like all good things, humour can go wrong.

It can at times, as Sigmund Freud knew, be the expression of hidden aggression. It was so with the terrible laughter attributed in the Old Testament to God who, from the heights of heaven, laughed men to scorn. The taunting laugh of adversaries, or the deep throated gloating laugh of proud and powerful people, is a very different thing from relaxed laughter with friends. Instead of diminishing hate and aggression, and releasing goodwill, laughter can in fact become a tool of mockery and malice. Instead of promoting humility it can be an expression of superiority, defiance and denigration. How hurtful the verbal sneer can be, compounded as it often is with contempt. Sneering requires no mastery of the facts. It begs every question. It both wounds and leaves a poison in the wound. The object of its sarcasm is left a laughing stock. I am sure it was this kind of chilling sneering laugh which prompted Jesus to say, 'Woe unto you who laugh now, you will weep'. At other times, laughter is a substitute for apologising for our failures. We speak of 'laughing something off'.

We don't have to teach children when to laugh. Young children laugh as birds sing. Their exuberance bursts forth into playfulness, smiles and carefree laughter. What we have to do is to teach them when *not* to laugh. In childish laughter there can be elements which we adults deem cruel. Studies have shown that what some young children find most amusing is someone else's suffering. They laugh at the misfit and those who deviate from the norm. The mother of a little Down's syndrome boy told me how upset she became when other children, for their entertainment, made him do silly things. Children also laugh when they gain a personal triumph over an adversary. 'I'm the king of the castle!' They laugh too when they see something demolished or kicked out of shape. Teenagers were recently arrested for pouring petrol over a cat and setting it on fire. The radio report of this sickening incident told how the boys stood back and laughed.

These characteristics of childish laughter were basic to the humour of many ancient peoples. They laughed at the misery of gladiators battling it out to death in the arena. The more blood spilt, the more they laughed. They laughed when they gained victory over enemies. They laughed at the mentally ill, at midgets and people with physical deformities. Circuses would employ dwarfs and people suffering from elephantiasis, a disease which causes the body to swell to enormous proportions. John Bunyan, of *Pilgrim's Progress* fame, tells of an ale-house owner who used his mentally handicapped son to entertain his guests. They would laugh at the boy's foolish words and gestures.

Though caustic laughter, of the kind uttered by Hitler when France finally surrendered, is still a favourite weapon of the immature, the coward and the snob, thankfully the majority of people feel there is something low about a person who derisively laughs at the sufferings, afflictions, failings, natural ignorance or innocence of others, who delights in 'man's inhumanity to man'. Laughter at people experiencing one disaster after another is today fortunately mainly confined to the stage or circus arena, or to the Tom and Jerry type of cartoon. In war comedies, like 'Dad's Army', 'M*A*S*H', 'Allo, Allo', conflicts are limited to shouts, growls, bluffs and fisticuffs, where no one gets seriously hurt. As well as taking on a windmill or two, the heroes have an amazing talent for running and hiding. I recall laughing heartily as I watched a Laurel and Hardy film in which the two heroes tried to plug a leak in a boat. The problem was that neither they, nor the hapless girl drowning with them, could agree which implements to use. Each was sure his or her remedy was the only one that would work. They finished up using the wood, tarpaulin and buckets to wallop each other, while they all sank into further disaster.

Thankfully the majority of those who today laugh at people's discomfiture and defeat, laugh only so long as no harm is done to the person, or no great loss sustained. We laugh to see the very properly dressed lady chasing her hat which has been blown off. But we would not laugh if she slipped and broke her leg, or if in the process she was hit by a passing car. The more immaculately dressed the lady, the faster she has to run, the more we laugh because the greater the incongruity. If it was a poor lady chasing a poor hat, it would not be funny.

During a morale boosting tour of American troops, General Eisenhower was due to address thousands of them lined up on the parade ground. Just before his arrival there was a heavy shower of rain. Soaked to the skin, the soldiers were in none too good humour. The General's speech did little to boost their morale. But as he left the raised platform, he slipped on the wet steps and finished up sitting on the muddy grass. As he picked himself up unharmed, gentle laughter was heard from the ranks of the soldiers. Turning to the accompanying officer, Eisenhower said, 'This has boosted their morale more than the speech'. The laughter of the soldiers arose from circumstances that involved discomfiture of an incongruous kind – a General, immaculately dressed, attended hand and foot, flat on his back; yet an incident, not involving sufficient distress to outweigh the pleasure of enjoying the incongruity of it.

It is a good general rule that if love does not prevail between you and others, think twice before you joke with them. If there is bad blood, your joke can so easily be interpreted as a 'dig'. Love makes us more sensitive as to when to use humour and when to refrain.

# Laughing at Nothing and at Everything

I HAVE long been wary of people who laugh at nothing, who are always serious and intense. Whereas those with a sense of humour readily acknowledge that they 'know in part and see only puzzling reflections in a mirror', those without a sense of humour are often convinced that they see clearly and know absolutely. They cannot tolerate any suggestion that they may not be right. Lacking the perspective which humour can bring, many militants and crusaders take themselves too seriously. They fail to see the absurdity of many of their pretensions, and their delusions of fame or grandeur. Their strong political, feminist, nationalist or religious convictions, translate themselves into intolerance and aggression, quarrels and confrontation. Konrad Lorenz has justification for saying in his book *On Aggression*, that the survival of civilisation depends to a significant degree upon our capacity for humour.

Within the church and many other organisations, numerous problems are created by humourless people who think that everything is a matter of life and death, and that every church battle is Armageddon. They get upset when not everyone falls into line when they blow the trumpet. I think of crusaders who make the monumental blunder of confusing seriousness with solemnity, and absolutists who are certain they have the truth and others do not. I think also of those very pious, ultra-serious folk in the church who are forever making a conscious effort to look redeemed, whose every gesture is pontifical, and whose voice goes plummy at the name of Jesus. Too often they dismiss as heretics all who do not think exactly as they do. Rigid and uncompromising, they are more concerned with the letter of the law than the spirit. It is difficult to imagine people with a sense of humour participating in the burning of other people at the stake, simply because they did not subscribe to a certain formulation of the doctrine of the Trinity, as happened in John Calvin's Geneva. Religious power without humour can be as dangerous as political power without honour. Laughter serves as a safety valve preventing seriousness from becoming absolute and faith from becoming bigotry.

The occasional flash of humour can enrich a sermon. I once used an Andy Capp strip cartoon to illustrate how hatred can consume and destroy those who harbour it. In the cartoon, Andy's boss kept slapping him across the chest whenever they met. Finally Andy had had enough. He said to his friend Amos, 'I am going to put a stick of dynamite in my shirt pocket. The next time he slaps me, he is going to get his hand blown off'. When rightly used, and not over-used, humour can be a powerful instrument in the service of truth.

I am also, however, wary of people who laugh at everything, people who are always funny and never serious, people who constantly employ humour to gain acceptance and admirers. Often the only thing they take with complete seriousness is themselves, their prestige and reputation. The comedian John Cleese tells how he once was a guest at a dinner party given by Peter Cook. 'For two and a half hours Peter made us laugh non-stop. After an hour I was tired laughing. I got the impression that night that Peter used humour to avoid making real contact with people.'

George Kaufmann, the distinguished theatre-director, said that whenever he saw three consecutive funny lines in a play, he stroked out two of them. Malcolm Muggeridge, writing of his years with the magazine *Punch,* said of his last day as

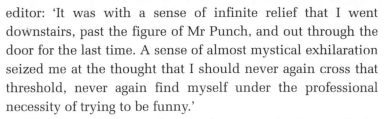

editor: 'It was with a sense of infinite relief that I went downstairs, past the figure of Mr Punch, and out through the door for the last time. A sense of almost mystical exhilaration seized me at the thought that I should never again cross that threshold, never again find myself under the professional necessity of trying to be funny.'

Likewise, when preachers endeavour to be funny all the time, they place an intolerable burden on themselves and their listeners. Poking fun at the incongruities on the surface of life is justified, provided we never forget that people need resources to deal with those which reach below the surface. It is a calamity when Andrew the comedian occupies the pulpit instead of Andrew the disciple, when the preacher is more intent on cracking jokes than on bringing people to a deeper understanding of God and the world.

IN a sermon on peace, Bishop Sherrill used humour to considerable effect. He was keen to point out how ridiculous it is to talk of peace as a generality. 'Everyone knows there is a difference between the peace of the lion that has just swallowed the lamb, and the peace of the lamb that has just been swallowed by the lion.'

I have often reminded those who think the world is going to the dogs that there has been no period in history when it has been very far from the kennels.

In the TV series 'Ever Decreasing Circles' one character was seen regularly resisting all efforts to make him prune the mountains of paper that swamped everything he did. 'What do you need that for?' he was asked with reference to some obscure bumph from an earlier decade. With great seriousness he replied, 'For filing' – an answer which many bureaucrats would accept as valid beyond question.

It is customary for the Moderator of the General Assembly of the Church of Scotland to bow each morning to the Assembly. The year James Harkness, the former Chaplain General, was Moderator, a commissioner was overheard to say, 'I never thought I would see the day when a General would bow to me, a lowly corporal'.

The Rev. Chaffey Moore, in his book *Reflections of an RAF Chaplain,* tells how as a young Anglican minister he was standing one day on a crowded platform at Lincoln station. When the train drew in, an elderly minister wearing a clerical collar stepped forward and invited him to join him in an empty carriage. Once in the carriage the old minister quickly lowered the window and, with rather a stern look, surveyed the passengers as they hurried past. Mr Moore saw them look up with expressions of alarm at the sight of this formidable clerical figure with the unsmiling face. Though the train was crowded, no one attempted to enter their carriage. Eventually, when the guard blew the whistle, the old minister pulled up the window and settled himself in the opposite corner. Surveying the empty carriage, he said, 'Thank God for the unpopularity of the Church of England'.

A man started giving cod-liver oil to his dog because he had been told it was good for dogs. He held the protesting dog's head between his knees, forced open its jaws and poured down the oil. One day the dog broke loose and spilled the oil. To his surprise the dog began licking it up. That was when he realised that the dog had been fighting not the oil, but his method of administering it. I often wonder if the explanation of the resistance of some people to the Gospel is similar?

The Rev. Archie Chisholm, formerly minister of Tummel and Loch Rannoch, tells of a conversation with his senior elder, a wise old man who had been a ploughman all his days, about a previous minister in the charge who had not only lacked tact, humour and commonsense, but seemed to rub everyone the wrong way. The congregation was dwindling fast. One Sunday, after an especially upsetting service and sermon, one of the elders remarked, 'He's an awful man. He should never have been a minister'.

'That may be true,' said the senior elder, 'but when you stop and think about it, what *else* would he have done?!'

A minister who preached on Psalm 119, verse 71 – 'It is good for me that I was afflicted' – illustrated his sermon by saying that whereas growth sometimes takes place best in sunlight, at other times a shady spot is preferable. He then continued, 'Whereas we plant roses where they will be exposed to sunshine, if we want fuchsias to do well we plant them in the shade'. After the sermon, from which he hoped some of his members would derive comfort, a lady thanked him profusely. His heart glowed until she added, 'Now I know what is wrong with my fuchsias'.

The Rev. Marc Carpenter tells how she once commented on the wonderful congregation there had been in a church in which she had been preaching. Her host laughed as he told her how, several weeks before, a minister who was convinced he was a legend in his own mind had been invited to preach. That day the congregation was rather thin. When he asked the minister at the end of the service if his coming had been announced the previous Sunday, the minister replied that it had not, but 'the congregation must have found out!'

In speaking about family life I often quote the novelist Penelope Fitzgerald. Once when asked in an interview if there was a fictional character with whom she specially identified, she replied, 'It changes as you get older. I used to weep for Romeo and Juliet. Now I think, their poor parents'.

The Danish philosopher Kierkegaard regularly poked fun at the incongruities of the established state church. He humorously highlighted the case of a man who was refused a licence to open a house of prostitution because he could not produce his baptismal certificate! In similar vein a Roman Catholic, with a twinkle in his eye, recently asked, 'Why is it lawful for a woman to avoid pregnancy by resorting to mathematics and physics, but not to chemistry?'

The daring Israeli attack on Entebbe airport resulted in the death of Jonathan Netanyahu. A collection of his letters was later published, *Self-Portrait of a Hero*. He tells how, just before the six-day war, an Englishman, an American and an Israeli were caught by a tribe of cannibals. Before being put into the pot, each was allowed a last wish. The Englishman asked for a whisky and got it, the American for a steak. The Israeli then asked the cannibal chief to kick him. At first he refused, but after much argument he did just that. At once the Israeli pulled out a gun and shot the cannibals. When the American and Englishman asked, 'If you had a gun all the time, why did you not shoot sooner?'

'Are you *crazy*?' said the Israeli. 'And have the United Nations call me an aggressor?'

During an election campaign, Harold MacMillan was approached by a lady who said, 'I would not vote for you if you were St Peter himself'.

'If I were St Peter,' came super Mac's reply, 'I doubt if you would be in my constituency.'

When a trendy minister invited his members to bring their favourite animal to church for an 'Animal Service', one farmer threatened to bring his bull.

Disraeli is quoted as having said that he did not object to
Gladstone having four aces up his sleeve, but he did object to
the idea that God put them there.

Ben Johnson, for many years minister at Inverkeithing, tells
of an experience he had one New Year's day. After breakfast
he took a walk down the town's main street. The shops were
all shut, and the curtains were still drawn in many homes.
Suddenly, round the corner into the deserted street came
two men singing with great gusto and walking in an erratic
manner. Though they stopped singing as they approached
him, they still swayed markedly. Then one of them said, 'My
goodness minister, are you no hame yet either?'

Dr Robert McCracken, who became the senior minister of the
Riverside Church in New York, began his ministry in
Glasgow. One day as he left the home of a member, he
noticed across the street his most critical member peering at
him from behind her curtains. To protect himself from yet
further criticism he decided to pay her a visit. But when he
knocked on the door there was no reply. So he stooped down
and looked through the keyhole. Lo and behold, staring back
at him was Mrs Maclean. Dr McCracken, who was seldom at
a loss for words, said, 'Mrs Maclean, this must be the first
time we have seen eye to eye'.

Dr Barclay's many books about the Bible and the Christian faith had a worldwide circulation. Having little interest in money, he was for a long time unaware how well off financially he had become. When a friend finally persuaded him to consult Tom McNaughton, a Glasgow accountant, about increased demands for income tax payments, Dr Barclay took with him a case crammed full of bank and royalty statements. Having glanced through the contents, Tom smiled and said, 'I wish now I had stuck in at Sunday School!'

# The Church
# and Humour

WILLIAM SHAKESPEARE made one of his characters, Sir Andrew Aguecheek, say, 'Methinks sometimes I have no more wit than a Christian has'. It saddens me that there is still often a strange absence of humour and joy in people's religion, and an absence of fun from the lives of very pious people. Too often in church circles the impression has been given that God is better pleased with tears than laughter, that the closer you get to godliness the more grimly sombre you become.

John Calvin, whose thinking exerted a considerable influence on Scottish religious thought, was not known for his exuberance or wit. I could not imagine anyone going to any of his numerous publications for a laugh. Calvin believed that whereas a dignified sober demeanour was evidence of a state of grace, laughter was evidence of our fallen nature. A book on Calvin's humour might well be one of the world's shortest. In the eighteenth and nineteenth centuries, a phrase like 'the tearful chidings of the ministry' was a more accurate description of the ministry than the 'cheerful tidings of the ministry'. During this period, the fourth Earl of Chesterfield wrote, 'There is nothing so illiberal and so illbred as audible laughter ... how low and unbecoming a thing laughter is: not to mention the disagreeable noise it makes, and the shocking distortion of the face that it occasions'.

The church's negative attitude to laughter continued for a long time. An old poem contains the lines:

*The Church meeting has begun*
*No more laughter, no more fun.*

In the early days of the Young Men's Christian Association, the magazine *Punch* was excluded from the Association's reading rooms because it was not sufficiently serious. The Scottish writer Eric Linklater told of a school report he was once given: 'He is doing fairly well, but is handicapped by a sense of humour.' A Dornoch man told me that the worst row he ever got as a boy was for laughing one Sunday afternoon at their dog which had got caught in a fishing net. The row was not for laughing at the plight of the dog, but for laughing on a Sunday. I can understand what prompted H L Mencken to define Puritanism as the haunting fear that someone somewhere might be happy. Now that is not a fair summing up of Puritanism, but there is an element of truth in it. The Puritans cast a disparaging eye on many of the the lighter and pleasanter aspects of life. Even the rejoicing associated in other countries with the great Christmas and Easter festivals was frowned on by the Kirk. Recalling his upbringing in Puritan New England, where for several years there was an aggressive crackdown on fun and laughter, Oliver Wendell Holmes said, 'I might have been a minister if a certain clergyman had not looked and talked so like an undertaker'.

Dr Marcus Dods, one of Scotland's most distinguished nineteenth century ministers, was almost not called to be minister of the Renfield Church in Glasgow because he had suggested that the Botanic Gardens in Edinburgh might be open for people to enjoy on a Sunday.

The Scottish poet John Ruskin was brought up in an extremely strict Calvinistic home. He tells how, when he was a boy, a relation gave him a toy jumping jack as a present. But his parents took it from him, declaring that such toys were not for a Christian child! In seventeenth century Scotland, dancing at weddings could result in a considerable fine. For a church member to be found in possession of a fiddle was a major offence in the eyes of the church courts. Though harps were associated with heaven, fiddles were regarded as instruments of the devil!

Nobody satirised the narrow Puritanical outlook on life better than Lord Neaves in his lyric entitled 'Saturday Night':

> *We zealots made up of stiff clay*
> *The sour looking children of sorrow*
> *While not over jovial today*
> *Resolve to be wretched tomorrow.*
> *We can't for a certainty tell*
> *What mirth may molest us on Monday,*
> *But at least to begin the week well*
> *Let us all be unhappy on Sunday.*

Though in the nineteenth century many eminent preachers like Charles Spurgeon were bright personalities with a keen sense of humour, their publishers, concerned to preserve the awe in which these princes of the pulpit were held, played down their cheerfulness and excised much of the humour from their printed sermons. Spurgeon, who believed ministers should radiate cheerfulness, was not happy that he should be so misrepresented. In a lecture he said, with tongue in cheek:

> *I don't believe in going about like some monks whom I saw in Rome, who salute each other in sepulchral tones, and convey the pleasant information, 'Brothers we must die!' To this lively salutation each lively brother of the order replies, 'Yes brother, we must die!' I was glad to be assured upon such good authority that all these lazy fellows are about to die. It is about the best thing they can do!*

It really is tragic that the Christian faith has at times been viewed by the world as an essentially grim and humourless affair, and Christians should be thought of as sad-faced people moving always with sober decorum. Writing of an African village, an anthropologist pointed out that before their conversion to Christianity, the villagers were noted for their hearty laughter, but after their conversion they displayed instead a nervous squeaky embarrassed laugh, what he called a 'mission giggle'.

It saddens me that some churches still seem only to succeed in converting cheerful sinners into miserable ones. Back of the frantic syncopations about 'the joy, joy, joy, we've got down in our hearts', there is too often a sepulchral seriousness about what goes on during the hour of worship.

In preparing for the Barclay lecture I visited the library of the divinity faculty of Edinburgh University. In the subject catalogue only one book was listed under the heading of 'Humour', and it was not even one of my own! I sometimes wonder if I would have fared better in the divinity library of Glasgow University. Had I discovered there a whole shelf of books on humour, I suspect some of those who regard laughter in church as inappropriate, might have seized on this as further proof that whereas Edinburgh University is often regarded as the theological centre of the Old world, and Princeton University the theological centre of the New world, Glasgow University is the theological centre of the Underworld! But that is to slander my own and Dr Barclay's fine *Alma Mater.*

In my theology studies at Glasgow we were encouraged to study the writings of the Swiss theologian Karl Barth and the American Reinhold Neibuhr, both of whom regarded humour as one of God's greatest gifts. Karl Barth spoke of laughter as being 'holy'. Writing of his prodigious theological efforts which resulted in twelve large volumes of Church Dogmatics, Barth said:

> *The angels laugh at old Karl. They laugh at him because he tries to grasp the truth about God in a book of Dogmatics. They laugh at the fact that volume follows volume and each is thicker than the previous one. As they laugh they say to one another, 'Look, here he comes now with his little push-cart full of volumes of the Dogmatics'.*

I further warmed to Barth when I heard how one day, in the grounds of Basle University, he was approached by an American student who inquired if by any chance he knew the world famous Karl Barth. With a twinkle in his eye, Barth replied, *'Know* him? I shave him every morning!'

What a lively sense of humour Reinhold Niebuhr also had. There was much laughter in his classes in Union Seminary, New York, where I studied for a year. He wrote movingly of the sound of 'laughter in the vestibule of the temple, and the echo of laughter in the temple itself'. On another occasion he said, 'Humour is a prelude to faith; and laughter is the beginning of prayer'. The New Testament professor C H Dodd was another scholar whose writings we studied at Trinity College. In fact I used to think a suitable motto for our Theological College might well have been a revised version of the great commandment, 'You shall love the Lord your *Dodd* with all your *Barth* and your *Niebuhr* as yourself'.

The idea that Christianity is incompatible with laughter and humour goes back a long way, to the early Church Fathers. Many of them distrusted laughter. Some taught that whereas God grants seriousness, it is the devil who bestows laughter. Clement of Alexandria, who wrote towards the end of the second century, regarded it as unthinkable that Christ should ever have laughed, for this would infer he had fallen from grace. In a sermon which Chrysostom delivered in Antioch in AD 390, he said:

> *The world is not a theatre in which we can laugh. We are not assembled together in order to burst into peals of laughter, but to weep for our sins. But some of you will want to say, 'I would prefer God to give me the chance to go on laughing and joking'. Is there anything more childish than thinking in this way? It is not God who gives us the chance to play, but the devil.*

Another Church Father, Ambrose, believed that 'jokes should be avoided even in small talk'. St Basil also admonished his followers to refrain from jesting. They were 'not to laugh or even suffer laugh-makers'. One of the principal rule-books for monks in the sixth century, the *Regula Magistri*, lists laughter as a despicable vice that wounds the soul. It is clear from this that early on, and for a long time afterwards, the church had little tolerance for what they regarded as the unsettling effects of laughter. 'What have we to do with tales and laughter?' wrote St Bernard. 'I judge that not only extravagant jesting is to be condemned, but *all* jesting.'

But despite the efforts of the early church to suppress laughter, it persisted. For a brief period in the Middle Ages the church admitted that certain forms of laughter were permissible. Some of the wandering friars began in fact to use humour in preaching, to catch the attention of passers-by, and sometimes to make a moral or theological point. Thomas Aquinas went much further in his *Summa Theologia* in the twelfth century. Far from just tolerating laughter and humour, he said that lack of humour is a sin – only a little sin perhaps, but nevertheless a sin. 'Good jokes,' he said, 'are to be appreciated.' The only stipulation Aquinas made was that jokes must not be against good behaviour, or be hurtful or degrading. Martin Luther's enthusiastic style and sense of humour are also well documented. Luther said, 'God is not a God of sadness and death. Christ is the Lord of joy; and so the Scriptures often say that we should rejoice. A Christian should and must be a cheerful person'.

Sir Thomas More, in the sixteenth century, had a lively sense of humour. He loved to goad and tease. In the history of laughter he is remembered as the one who converted the word *geste* – 'story'– into the word 'jest' in its modern sense. Witty anecdotes enliven his writings. To the dismay of many in the church, he gathered round him many other wits. The crown and the church became more and more concerned about their lack of sobriety. During his time in the Tower of London on charges of treason, More's writings suddenly turned dramatically sombre. One wonders if he was brainwashed into writing from prison, 'Life is no laughing time, but rather a time of weeping .... Our Saviour left us no example of laughing, but he left us an example of weeping'. I hint at this possibility of pressure being put on Thomas More, because the church seems to have felt that if it could gag him, his witty friends might be frightened into stark sobriety. If the anecdotes about More's execution in 1535 are true, he seems to have recovered his cheerfulness and sense of humour before mounting the scaffold. On having his soul commended to God by the chaplain, Thomas More said he was sure God would not refuse one who was so joyfully anticipating seeing him. We are told More accepted help climbing up on to the scaffold, but joked that, 'As for coming down I will fend for myself'. He is reported also to have asked the executioner to let the axe spare his beard since 'it at least had not offended King Henry'.

A SMALL boy was told by his mother that his great aunt had died, an aunt who had a reputation for seldom smiling, being rather grouchy and not too fond of children. Her religion was for the most part one of doom and gloom. When the boy's mother informed him that Aunt Gladys had gone to heaven to be with God, he responded with a sincere look of sympathy, 'Poor God'.

During a Moderatorial visit to the Western Isles, I expressed surprise to the Presbytery Clerk of Lewis that a Kirk Session should frown on a minister enjoying a coffee in his garden on a Sunday afternoon.

'Moderator,' he said, 'not even the midges come out in Stornoway on a Sunday afternoon.'

St Theresa of Avila prayed to be delivered from sour vinegary Christians.

Of a strict Calvinistic elder it was said, 'He had a face like the edge of a hatchet dipped in vinegar'.

An American minister told me of preaching many years ago in a Perthshire church. The humorous remarks he made at the beginning of the service fell on stony ground. No one smiled or laughed. He later apologised to two of the members. He explained that in his American church, people often laughed at the occasional humorous story or remark.

'Oh we enjoyed your humour,' they said. 'We just didn't think it right to show it.'

Like the composer Haydn, I believe God will forgive me if I serve him cheerfully.

When a minister asked some children, 'What it does it mean to be holy?', one little boy said, 'To do what Mum asks the first time she asks'.

Dr McAfee Brown tells how, in the old days in the Southern Presbyterian Church in the United States, one of the questions asked of students who were to be licensed to preach was, 'Are you prepared to be damned for the glory of God?'

A student who had been grilled for an hour by a very conservative Presbytery, was finally allowed by only two votes to proceed to licensing. When asked, during the service which followed, if he was prepared to be damned for the glory of God, he replied, 'I am prepared to go further than that. I am prepared to have this whole Presbytery damned for the glory of God!'

John Levack tells how, when he was studying divinity at Trinity College, it was customary when lunch was over for one of the students to make a speech which usually ended by accusing someone of some peccadillo, real or imaginary. It was then the person's duty to reply. It was all done in good humour. The idea was to accustom future ministers to the art of public speaking.

One occasion stuck in John Levack's memory. It concerned a James Macdonald, a shy Highlander. The 'moral censor' that day said, 'It has come to my knowledge that James has become engaged. What I would like to know is how he came to have the courage to propose?'

James slowly rose to his feet. 'Gentlemen, I should perhaps explain that I have known Mary for a long time. We lived in the same village, went to school together, and our parents are good friends. I recently felt she was the woman I wanted to marry. After the service one Sunday we came out of church together. I took her over to a corner of the churchyard where my ancestors are buried. 'Mary,' I said, 'my grandfather and grandmother lie there. My father and mother will lie there in due course, and I presume that when the time comes, I will lie there too. Mary, how would you like to lie there some day?'

For many years Charles Spurgeon was involved in running a small Pastor's College in England. One day, during a preaching seminar, Spurgeon gave a text to each of the students. They were then given a few minutes to gather their thoughts before preaching briefly on it.

The first student, having climbed the steps into the wooden pulpit, said, 'The subject I have been given is Zaccheus. There are three things I would point out about Zaccheus. First, he was a very little man and so am I. Second,

Zaccheus was up a tree, and at this moment I am also up in what was once a tree. Third, we are told that Zaccheus made haste to come down, and so will I.'

As the young man left the pulpit, Spurgeon, who had a lively sense of humour, was heard to say, 'Young man, you will do alright'.

Spurgeon also told of a farmer who complained that at an afternoon service, one of Spurgeon's students had preached far too long. 'He ought to have given over at four o'clock, but he kept on till half-past, and there were my cows waiting to be milked! How would he have liked it if he had been a cow?'

'I agree,' said Spurgeon 'the society for the Prevention of Cruelty ought to have prosecuted that young sinner. How can farmers hear to profit when they have cows on the brain?'

# The Joy and
# Humour of Jesus

THE picture of Jesus – as one given to weeping but not to laughing, as one given always to serious discourse – has unfortunately taken root in the minds of many. I wonder if one of the reasons for this is that, in the Gospels, the tragic events of Holy Week are related so fully that reading the Gospels we might picture them as the story of Jesus' tragic and brutal death with some introductory passages added. Not surprisingly therefore, many picture Jesus as primarily a man of sorrows. But this misrepresents the Christ portrayed in the earlier chapters, who likened himself and his disciples to a bridal party. The early Christians were described by their contemporaries as '*hilares*' – cheerful. There was about them a certain holy hilarity. They obviously smiled and laughed often. Joy was such a dominant theme of Jesus' teaching, that G K Chesterton said 'joy is the gigantic secret of the Christian'. Jesus, far from being a kill-joy, *wanted* people to enjoy life to the full. 'I am come that you might have life and have it more abundantly' – not moribundantly. His joy and love of life were as striking as his compassion.

I sometimes wonder what effect a verse in Luke's Gospel (6: 25) had on the the early church's thinking about humour, a verse where Jesus is quoted as saying, 'Woe unto you who laugh now, you shall mourn and weep'. That verse certainly had a devastating effect on the thinking of the atheistic philosopher Nietzche. He wrote, 'What has so far been the greatest sin here on earth? Was it not the word of him who said, "Woe unto those who laugh here?"' .... Then Nietzche added, 'Jesus did not love enough, else he would have loved us who laugh'. Had Nietzche studied more closely the context of this saying of Jesus, and the overall picture which the Gospels give us of Jesus, I don't think he would have written that. I am certain Jesus was speaking here about cruel, arrogant laughter directed against others – the humour of hate, of cynicism, racial prejudice, tasteless humour, inappropriate humour, sick and malicious humour, and humour that is a tool of arrogance and aggression. I am sure it was cruel laughter that prompted Jesus to say, 'Woe unto you who laugh now, you will weep'.

Had Jesus been opposed to all laughter, as Nietzche inferred, would he have said, as recorded a few verses earlier in Luke's Gospel, 'Happy are you who weep now, you will laugh'? Jesus himself used humour and mild irony to season serious discourse, to pierce illusion and hypocrisy and get to the heart of truth. What a pity that a wink cannot make its way on to the printed page, for I am sure Jesus often winked as he drew word pictures of people lighting lamps and putting them under buckets or beds, as he poked fun at people trying to remove a speck from someone else's eye with a great log in their own, meticulously cleaning the outside of the cup while leaving the inside dirty, or walking miles in the wilderness to see a reed shaken by the wind. I think also of the picture he painted of the religious leaders of his day straining at gnats in their soup and then swallowing a camel – humps, feet and all.

On another occasion he spoke of the fabricated excuses people offer for not following him, to cover up the real reason. He told them a story about three men and the excuses they offered for not coming to the landlord's evening party. One man had bought a piece of land and had to go and see it. The second had bought a set of oxen and had to try them out. To see the irony in that, make a list of the number of people you know who would buy a piece of property or cattle without first seeing them. The third man's excuse was that he had married a wife. To us that seems more reasonable. Today many men resolve before they get married to be the boss in their own home, or else they will know the reason why. But after marriage they usually *know* the reason why. One husband said, 'My wife leads a double life – hers and mine'. But in the Jewish household the male made all the major decisions, and even if he did not, was not likely to broadcast the fact. You can sense Jesus' irony throughout the entire parable.

When the disciples James and John were lobbying for the box seats in the coming kingdom, and there was obviously the prospect of a bitter row with the other disciples, I can well imagine Jesus seeking to diffuse the situation by gentle humour, saying, 'Now then, you two sons of thunder'.

It is significant also that Jesus' watchword was '*tharsete*' – our 'cheer up'. He criticised the Jewish leaders for their long glum faces, as though in mourning for their faith. People wanted Jesus with them, not only in times of sadness and sickness, but also as guest at their wedding banquets. Everyone wanted to hang out with him. He was the Lord of the Wedding Supper as well as the Last Supper. Had Jesus been a lean ascetic with a sombre face, one who despised the good things of this world, he would not have been invited. That he and his disciples enjoyed festivities and parties scandalised the religious people of his day. His words and actions were a striking contrast to the serious conventional piety of the Pharisees. The difference was like a dirge to a dance. He did not fit the picture they had of what a preacher or prophet should be like. They thought he was too cheerful to be a holy man.

Has it ever struck you how many of Jesus' parables were about parties? The foolish virgins missed the party. The man without the wedding garments missed the party because he was too pompous to accept the appropriate clothing, freely offered. The elder brother missed the music, dancing and feasting because he was angry and would not go in. The famous prodigal son story is basically a parable about the nature of God, a God who not only forgives but says, 'Let us be merry'. Jesus contrasted himself with the very straight-laced John the Baptist. Unfortunately some of his followers have been better followers of John the Baptist than Jesus, better followers of Calvin than Luther.

I find it significant that the poet Dante, who likened heaven and hell to multi-storey buildings, consigned the sullen to the lowest region of hell. His reason was that they were so doggedly sad in the face of God's sweet air. Dante, on the other hand, said of the eighth level of heaven, 'I seemed to see the universe alight with a single smile'.

Dietrich Bonhoeffer coined the phrase, 'the Church for fun'. I wish it had caught on, like his arresting description of Jesus as 'the man for others'. The church's image needs such a face-lift. To be on the side of kindly fun and laughter is an important aspect of the Christian way of life. I believe we misrepresent Jesus when we refuse to share, care and forgive; but we also misrepresent him when we don't smile and laugh, when we make our religion a thing of doom and gloom, or when we take ourselves too seriously. The Bible tells us that in heaven there will be no more tears. Thank goodness it does not say that about spontaneous and kindly laughter.

MANY have forgotten that Isaiah contemplated a joyful Messiah: 'The spirit of the Lord is upon me. He has sent me to bring glad tidings to the lowly, to heal the broken-hearted ... to give them the oil of gladness in place of mourning, the glorious mantle instead of a listless spirit'.

During my year as Moderator, I found it helpful to keep reminding myself that when Jesus rode into Jerusalem on the back of a donkey, and everyone was waving palm branches and singing, the donkey never for a moment thought the praise and accolades were actually for him.

One Easter a man complained that every time he came to church he had to sing the same hymns. 'It is always either *Jesus Christ is Risen Today* or *Still the Night*.'

The day I most dread is the day I fill up my tax return. I sometimes feel it would be a lot quicker and easier, like Mary and Joseph, to go to Bethlehem.

The word 'suffer', as used in the King James Bible's translation of Jesus' famous saying, 'Suffer the little children to come unto me', is less precise than the modern translation, 'Let the children come … ' – but is there not a sense in which little children have at times *to be suffered?* I think of when they are tired and fractious, or wake up early. Emblazoned on the T-shirt of an angelic sleeping toddler were the words, 'Nobody knows the trouble I've been'. The manufacturer knew that being a parent is not all sweetness.

When the mother of John Wesley was asked, 'Why do you tell that child a thing twenty times', Susannah replied, 'Because nineteen times are not enough'.

Mark Twain tells of a service he attended in Hartford, where the preacher was a missionary home from Africa:

> *His voice was beautiful. He told of the sufferings of the natives. He pleaded for help with such moving simplicity that I mentally doubled the fifty cents I had intended to put in the plate. As the address proceeded, describing so pitifully the misery of the natives, the dollar in my mind gradually rose to five dollars. A little further along the missionary had me crying. I felt that all the cash I had with me would be insufficient, and decided to write a large cheque. But as that preacher went on and on, I abandoned the idea of a cheque. Later I got back to five dollars – four, three, two, one. Still he went on. When the plate came round, I took two cents out of it.*

I am sure Jesus would have sympathised with Mark Twain. He kept reminding his religious contemporaries that they would not be heard for their much-speaking.

Jesus enjoyed the company of children. I can imagine him also enjoying their unconscious humour.

A three year old looked out of the window and saw lightning for the first time. 'Grandma,' he shouted, 'God just took my picture!'

Dr Wright, from Lochgelly in Fife, tells how one Christmas their minister asked the children if they could tell him what would have been different if Jesus had not been born that first Christmas. He was sure they would say they would not get any Christmas presents. But instead a ten year old said, 'Sir, you would not have a job'.

When a pre-school teacher was asked one day by a child in her class how old she was, not wanting to reveal her true age she replied 'thirty-five'.

The child's eyes widened with amazement, 'Wow, you're older than Jesus'.

A little boy reciting the Lord's Prayer was heard to say, 'Give us this day our day in bed'.

The Rev. Ian Roy tells of two boys who had each been given a goldfish. One morning it was discovered that the goldfish belonging to the younger boy was dead. The older boy sought to comfort his younger brother by saying that it was all right, that his gold fish had gone to be with Jesus.

'Oh not that man,' said the little boy, becoming even more distraught. 'He will feed him to the five thousand.'

A little girl was likewise distraught when her cat was hit by a passing car and died. Her mother, seeking to console her, said, 'Well at least you know your cat is now with God'.

The girl screwed up her face, thought for a minute and then said, 'I don't think so. What would God want with a dead cat?'

A wee girl excitedly told her aunt who was visiting, 'That's *our* church – the building with the plus sign on the roof'.

Shortly after the Morgan family moved in, their four year old son stopped his tricycle outside a neighbour's garden.

'How are you today, Mr Morgan?' asked the neighbour.

'I'm fine, thank you.'

Then, looking puzzled, the wee lad asked, 'Did you think I was my father?'

An inexperienced teacher stood at the blackboard writing down the Ten Commandments as the class called them out.

'Keep Sunday holy,' said one.

Another said, 'You shall not steal'.

'Don't commit adultery,' said another.

'What's adultery?' came the question she hoped would not be asked.

With great presence of mind she replied, 'Adultery is when a male and a female live together, but are not married'.

A silence followed. The explanation seemed to satisfy.

'Any more commandments?'

'Don't tell lies,' said a boy.

She breathed a sigh of relief. The crisis was past. But then another boy raised his hand and said, 'I live with my mother and we're not married. Are *we* committing adultery?'

When a city teacher one day brought a neighbour's pet rabbit to show the children, they asked all kinds of questions. The young teacher became slightly flustered when one boy asked if it was a boy or a girl rabbit. When she admitted she did not know, a little girl said, 'We could take a vote on it'. Gallup poll biology!

The school chaplain was speaking about the importance of honesty. What he did not know was that at the Assembly the previous day, the headmaster had spoken sternly to the children about not dropping crisp packets and sweetie papers in the playground, but placing them instead in the litter bins provided.

When, during his talk, the chaplain said, 'Suppose you were walking along the street behind me and I dropped a ten pound note, what would you do?'

An eager hand shot up, 'Please sir, I would pick it up and put it in the litter bin'.

The Rev. George Barr tried an alphabetical quiz with his Sunday school. He asked them to suggest fruits or flowers beginning with the different letters. For 'Q' one little boy suggested 'cucumber'.

# The Divine Comedy

IN the literature of great comedy, giants regularly become dwarfs, the high and mighty get their come-uppance, and Cinderellas are fitted with glass slippers. Clowns and comedians delight in collapsing the pedestals upon which the elite, the phony and the self-righteous position themselves. I have entitled this chapter 'The Divine Comedy', for time and time again it is the incongruous and the unexpected which characterise the Gospel story. The folly of human pride and pretension, a regular theme of humourists, is also a common theme of the Bible. The Genesis story of men building the Tower of Babel, 'whose top would reach the heavens', contains flashes of divine humour. The tower is so minute from the perspective of heaven, that God has to 'come down' to see it! 'Whoever exalts himself will be humbled,' said Jesus, 'and whoever humbles himself will be exalted.' In the Gospels swollen egos are often deflated, and people high up the pecking order are rendered powerless.

Paul spoke of the foolishness of the wise and the wisdom of the foolish. He called on his contemporaries to be fools and failures for Christ's sake. He wanted them to work for the fulfilment of God's purposes, not necessarily to work them out. Jesus himself was a failure, but a failure to the glory of God. Not many of the members of the early Church were well-educated, influential or of noble birth. They were for the most part humble folk. Having said that, we must remember that the humble are not shy people who hate the limelight or avoid controversy. Jesus showed a confidence that had no trace of inferiority. The truly humble have little or no interest in the question of superiority or inferiority. They are free to be of help to others, free to speak up for others, free to see the good and worth in others. Those on the other hand who have too high or too low an opinion of themselves, have this in common – the horizon of their concern seldom extends beyond themselves.

Could anything be more incongruous than God choosing to reveal himself through one born in the donkey's quarters behind a cheap motel, in a fifth rate corner of the Roman Empire. What divine comedy, God revealing his awesome power through human weakness, his incredible love through mortal suffering, his infinite greatness in lowly acts of service. In the Gospels the incongruity is there from first page to last. At the end of a brief ministry, Jesus is strung up for all the wrong reasons. He is put to death as a nationalist revolutionary when the only revolution he was after was a revolution of the human heart. His burning concern is for the well-being of all nations. He was in fact so much a citizen of the world that few today think of him as a Jew.

The Gospel story is full of comic reversals. One might have imagined the Messiah picking a dream team comprising the brightest Rabbis, and the best business minds. But Jesus did not choose those who looked for answers in text-books or pocket-books. Instead he picked apparent losers, and those with little to lose. Jesus had little interest in people's consuming concern with such categories as important and unimportant, winners and losers, rich and poor, somebodies and nobodies. He had no time for the mental yardsticks with which we constantly measure other people – status, power, appearance, wealth, career achievements.

In an Upper Room in Jerusalem the disciples were so preoccupied with who was the greatest that they refused to undertake the foot-washing. They were on their way to becoming rulers, not servants. Jesus on the other hand, unconcerned about self-image, took the pitcher and the towel and did what they refused to do. On another occasion he interrupted their jealous dispute by saying, 'The leader must be like the servant'. We find the same comic reversal in the episode in which women brought their children to Jesus that 'he might touch them'. Jesus' disciples were certain Jesus had more important things to do than pay attention to small children. But when the disciples attempted to send them away, Jesus said indignantly, 'Let the children come to me, do not hinder them; for to such belongs the kingdom of God'. Because Jesus was not interested in the question of where people stood on some human pyramid, they deemed him crazy. The novelist Dostoevsky seems to have understood this comic reversal, for he entitled a novel about Christ, *The Idiot*.

People often approach the Bible with such deadly seriousness that they miss the laughter and the comedy. New Testament scholars have for example long puzzled over how to interpret Jesus' strange conversation with the Canaanite woman (Matthew 15: 21-28). I believe a lot of kidding was going on. Jesus was joking with her, and she responded in jest. Luke recounts the great prank God played on the intelligentsia of this world (Matthew 11: 25). 'I thank you Father, Lord of heaven and earth, because you have hidden these things from the wise and the intelligentsia and have revealed them to infants … ', to untutored folk in the villages rather than the learned scribes and scholars in the synagogues. What mischievous gratitude.

The Gospel is about an unknown nobody from nowhere of importance, disclaiming conventional rules of protocol, exposing the hypocrisies of the self-righteous and revealing the virtues of rogues, defying every earthly power, rewriting religion, reversing values, proclaiming hope to those who had no hope, refusing to accept that the gravedigger and the undertaker have the last word. The Gospel is about the out-landishness or preposterousness of God who does apparently crazy and impossible things with despised and apparently impossible people. It is harder, said Jesus, for a rich person to enter Paradise than, as we might say, for Ted Turner or Andrew Carnegie to get through a night deposit slot at the bank. But then, Jesus immediately added, though for man it is impossible, for God all things are possible, because God is the master of the impossible.

The law in Jesus' day said, 'Keep your distance from lepers and sinners'; but Jesus unhesitatingly touched lepers, and invited Zaccheus, the most despised man in the village, to share a meal with him. It was all so outrageous. His remarks, as he stood at the door of the temple, were also unexpected. That day, some of the worshippers put in very considerable sums. But Jesus' attention was focussed on a woman whom no one else noticed — a poor widow struggling to make ends meet. She was perhaps embarrassed to have only two of the smallest coins in circulation to contribute. But surprise, surprise, Jesus called attention to her generosity: 'This poor widow has put in more than all those who are contributing to the treasury. For they all contributed out of their abundance; but she, out of her poverty, has put in everything she had' (Mark 12: 43,44). It was literally her next meal. By the comparative standards of the secular world, Jesus' evaluation is nonsense. Such a method of calculation would guarantee a stock-market crash. Yet there is a foolishness here which is wiser than the wisdom of men.

Many of Jesus' parables must have electrified those who first heard them. The themes are daring, the dramatic turns and twists sudden and surprising. Many of them resemble holy jokes. I wonder if that is why Jesus seemed reluctant to explain them. If you have to explain a joke you might as well save your breath. In one parable he likens God to a man who, when his friend comes knocking at midnight, says, 'Be quiet. You will wake the children'. When the friend pays no heed, but goes on leaning on the doorbell, the man finally staggers down the stairs and gives him what he wants, to be rid of him. In the parable of the Good Samaritan, a parable about the place of the despised in God's scheme of things, he chose as the hero the least likely candidate – a member of a despised race. Not surprisingly many of his listeners, for whom the phrase 'Good Samaritan' was a complete contradiction, found it quite shocking. It simply could not be that a Samaritan, the despised of the earth, could possibly have a role in God's purposes.

Another familiar collapsing of categories is contained in Jesus' parable of the Pharisee and the tax-gatherer who went up to the temple to pray. The righteous Pharisee was the kind of person who could strut even when sitting down. He would fain have made a 'closed shop' of God's kingdom. He would have excluded all who did not measure up to his standards. In the temple he proudly thanks God he is not like other men – 'extortioners, unjust, adulterers, or even like this tax collector'. The tax-gatherer on the other hand cries out, 'God be merciful to me a sinner!' To Jesus the Pharisee's virtue was so cankered by pride that it was almost rotten, and the tax-gatherer's transgressions were so saved by humility that they were well-nigh forgotten.

So many of Jesus' parables, like the one about the unjust steward, don't fit our expectations. Preachers are strongly tempted to turn the page and look for another from which to preach. The parable about the workers in the vineyard also stops us dead in our tracks. At the end of the day those who had worked only one hour receive the same pay as that promised to those who had worked since dawn. The story is not intended to teach us economics. It is a parable about the extravagant generosity of a God who refuses to have his generosity limited. In the parable no one receives from God's hand less than God has promised. Many receive more.

I sometimes wonder if we miss the deeper incongruity of the parable of the lost sheep. I suspect Jesus' original audience grasped it. No shepherd in his right mind in Palestine would have left 99 sheep unattended in what the Bible tells us was 'open pasture', where wild beasts roamed. Unattended sheep would have wandered off in many different directions. The entire flock might have been lost for the sake of one sheep. I believe Jesus was once again deliberately making the point that the love of God bucks the anticipated order. It is reckless, high risk. Certainly that is the message of the story which follows, about the rebellious son who is given a party, and a dutiful son who sits outside and simmers. There are two prodigals in this story, the first being the son who blows his inheritance on liquor and sex. The second is the father. Was there ever such prodigal love? He runs to meet his returning son, even though we are told oriental noblemen never ran. Instead of experiencing the ruthless hostility he deserves, the son is confronted with an incredible, and totally unexpected, demonstration of love. The love expressed is too profound for words. To begin with, his father's eyes and welcoming hug speak for his tongue. Only later does he say, 'Fetch the best robe'. That would be the father's own robe which was kept for grand occasions. 'Kill the fatted calf.' God says Jesus is like that crazy father, that reckless shepherd.

Another parable depicts God as the eccentric host who, when the 'green wellie brigade' all have more important things to do than accept his invitation to dinner, goes out and invites those living in cardboard boxes and eating at soup kitchens to join him at the banquet table. I like to imagine that when they had all gathered, the musicians in the gallery played 'Amazing grace'.

FOR many years David Reid was minister of Helensburgh Old. At the induction of his friend and colleague Fred Booth to a neighbouring church, David was invited to speak. That night he warned the congregation against expecting Fred to usher in the Kingdom single-handed. 'After all,' he said with a twinkle in his eye, 'Whoever heard of a Messiah named Fred?'

Fred said later that had he known at the time that the root meaning of Frederick was 'one who rules in peace', he would have pointed out in his reply, that it would not really have been so incongruous for the Messiah to be called Fred.

During Advent a primary school teacher asked the class what baby Jesus' mother was called.

'Mary, Mary,' they answered excitedly.

When she then asked them the name of baby Jesus' father, one little boy said, 'Was it Virg?'

When the surprised teacher asked why he thought that, the wee lad replied, 'Because we are told that the Virg and Mary had a baby boy'.

'I have never heard a sermon from which I did not receive some good,' said a fine old man. 'But I have had many near misses!'

A well-educated woman asked her minister if she could have a copy of the sermon he had preached on the doctrine of the Trinity. The minister was thrilled until she added, 'I just didn't understand it at all'.

During a children's address in a country church the minister asked the children, 'Why do you think the shepherd in Jesus' story left the ninety-nine sheep to go and look for the one that had got lost?'

He did not get the answer he expected. 'Please sir, it was probably the tup!' [the ram]

In the Highlands the shepherd and his dog will often finish a long day on the hills exhausted, but not a sheep will be lost. A poetic Highland preacher once elaborated on this fact. The lilt in his voice added force and tenderness to his words. 'The Lord is my shepherd. Aye and more than that, he has two collie dogs named Goodness and Mercy. With the Good Shepherd before, and them behind, even poor sinners like you and me can hope to win home at the last.'

A misprint in a hymn highlighted the essential message of the New Testament. Instead of reading 'There is a wideness in God's mercy like the wideness of the sea', it read 'There is a wildness in God's mercy, like the wildness of the sea'.

Golda Meir once said to some of her fellow politicians: 'Don't be humble. You are not that great.'

When John Cleese was asked if he could make God laugh, he replied: 'Yes, I could tell him my plans.'

Lois Self tells how, when her sister Marilyn was seven, her Sunday school teacher told the class that the following week she wanted them to write out the Twenty-third Psalm from memory. Marilyn did it perfectly until she reached the end. Then instead of writing 'Surely goodness and mercy shall follow me', she wrote 'Surely to goodness Mercy shall follow me all the days of my life'.

John Levack tells how the much-loved parish priest of Greenock, Father Daniel, invited several other Greenock ministers to a lecture given by a prominent Biblical scholar. His address was entitled 'The Apostle to the Gentiles'. A week later they and other Renfrewshire ministers met at the launch of a new ship at the Greenock shipyard. Present also that day was Robert McNeil, the minister of Kilmacolm, a most desirable residential area not far from Greenock.

Realising that Father Daniel had not met Robert, John Levack said, 'May I introduce Bob McNeil, the minister of Kilmacolm Parish?'

'Ah,' said Father Daniel, 'you'll be the Apostle to the Genteel'.

# What makes us laugh?

IN this book I have dealt only with sincere laughter, not that which has the sound of counterfeit coins. Laughter associated with nervous, insecure people, or sounded forth to attract attention or to impress others, is outwith my remit. So also is hysterical laughter and laughter induced by excessive drinking.

Though what makes us laugh ultimately defies analysis, one factor is the discrepancy between the people we are and might be. Comedy is about imperfection, about how far short people fall from perfection. It is also about the incongruous and unexpected – hearing a small child use an adult phrase correctly, or seeing a St Bernard and a chihuahua walking side by side.

The Rev. Uist Macdonald tells of conducting worship in Govan Old Church. During the worship service a man, who had obviously passed the 'pint' of no return in a nearby pub, entered the sanctuary. His footsteps were audible as he staggered on the stone floor. A few seconds later his pal, also the worse for wear, opened the back door and shouted, 'Jimmy, I told you this is no the Lyceum'. It was all so incongruous and unexpected that the congregation not surprisingly laughed.

The popularity with infants of the rattle and the modern equivalents of the Jack in the Box and squeaking dolls, stems also from the surprise factor. Is it because we cannot surprise ourselves that we cannot tickle ourselves? Many people laugh when they first see themselves in convex and concave mirrors, but if this was a daily occurrence they would no longer laugh. The element of surprise would have gone. Children often laugh when they see an ostrich for the first time. Youngsters at a school in Malawi laughed heartily when they saw and touched my wife's curly silver hair. They had not seen the like before. One hundred and fifty years previously they laughed when they first saw a white person, but whenever that became a regular occurrence they stopped laughing.

Recall Charlie Chaplin's brilliant portrayal of the Tramp – his clipped moustache and soulful eyes, his shabby but once elegant clothes, his unique walk, his dusty dignity. The Tramp combined in his costuming clothes from both ends of the social spectrum. The aristocratic bowler hat, bow tie and dress coat contrasted sharply with the floppy shoes and baggy pants of the typical street beggar. Millions of early film-goers loved the Tramp and laughed at his antics and problems. He was a somebody and a nobody at the same time. Most comic duos today embrace the same two extremes. In the television comedies 'The Two Ronnies', 'Little and Large', and 'Alas Smith and Jones', the big guy is forever trying with verbal right hooks to get the better of the small guy. The contrast is just as great between Oliver and Hardy – Stan overweight and over-bearing, Laurel almost anorexic and brow-beaten; Eric More-cambe the witty bungling fool and Ernie Wise the dapper ladies' man; Peter Cook the unattractive know-all and Dudley Moore the smaller loveable innocent.

The unexpected and incongruous are also essential elements of the joke. One thinks one knows the track a story is taking and then suddenly it is derailed. A few examples will illustrate this.

A WEALTHY American gentleman in his mid-seventies returned one spring from a winter sojourn in Florida engaged to a beautiful twenty-nine year old girl. When one of his friends asked him how he had got such a lovely young woman to agree to marry him, he replied, 'It was quite simple. I told her I was ninety-four!'

An elderly episcopal minister was having difficulty recalling the names even of people he had known for a long time. One day he noticed a colleague coming towards him in the superstore, a minister he knew well, but whose name he could not remember. As they approached he put out his hand to greet his colleague. As he did so he walked into a mirror. The older you become the more truth there is in the young lad's definition of memory as 'something you forget with'.

When a businessman told his friend he had not spoken to his wife for a whole week, the friend inquired if it had been a major row.

'Oh nothing like that,' said the man. 'I just didn't like to interrupt.'

The father of four sons was desperate to have a daughter. When their fifth child was born a girl, he quickly left the labour suite and went to his local pub to celebrate. When one of his friends asked who the baby was like, he replied, 'I never looked at the face!'

Illustrating how a great deal of Jewish humour is about money, Rabbi Blue told of a Jew who had been knocked down by a car. Having wrapped him in a blanket and put a pillow under his head, one of the paramedics inquired if he was comfortable. 'Oh,' said the Jew, 'I make a living.'

The dedication in Albert Malvino's book *Electronic Principles* reads: 'To Joanna, my brilliant and beautiful wife, without whom I would be nothing. She always comforts and consoles, never complains or interferes, asks nothing, endures all, and writes my dedications.'

DR ANDREW Herron told how he once had to cancel a holiday trip to Switzerland because both he and his wife had succumbed to a serious bout of 'flu'. Their holiday fortnight was spent crawling in and out of bed. At a Kirk social which he had agreed to chair shortly after the intended date of his return, he thought he had better explain their lack of suntan. In his opening remarks, he told how he had pinned a notice to their door: *We have not flown; we have 'flu'.*

A few days later he overheard a lady who had been present that night, and who had thought it an extraordinarily funny joke, repeat it to a friend. But the way she put it was: *We have not flown; we have the 'flu'.*

Not surprisingly her friend saw nothing to laugh at.

Likewise, if the teller of an anecdote forestalls the unexpected ending, the joke falls flat. That is when the experienced comedian will pull out a face-saver such as, 'My wife told me that story would never work. I see you all side with her'.

Sometimes, to heighten the incongruity, the story is tagged on to some celebrity – a Prime Minister, celebrated film star or sportsman. The comic dictionary defines an anecdote as a brief account of an incident that never actually occurred in the life of a famous person. That is to overstate the case, but there is an element of truth in it.

Whereas you find pranks and jokes in the kindergarten, you do not find wit. Wit comes from the old English word '*witan*', to know. It implies the exercise of the intellect. It lies in the province of manipulating language. The element of surprise is sublimated to a higher level. Commonplace words and phrases end with an unexpected twist. As well as amusing us, witty remarks give us something to muse on.

Whereas the great Shakespearean tragedies deal with the affairs of kings and queens, noble lords and ladies – King Lear, Macbeth, Julius Caesar – Shakespeare's comedies belong to the

common people, to the world of money-lenders, taverns ....
'The Taming of the Shrew', 'As you like it', 'Comedy of Errors',
'Much Ado about Nothing'. Still the best comedians are keen
observers of life. They see incongruities and humour in
ordinary situations and extract laughter from the small-change
of life. Wit is truth brought alive by a fertile imagination.

*   *   *

Experience is something you don't get until after you need it.

The hardness of the butter is proportional to the softness of
the bread.

Have you noticed that when you wash tight clothes they get
tighter, but when you wash loose clothes they get looser.

The further the seat from the aisle in the theatre, the later its
occupant arrives.

Counting calories has become for many a weigh of life.

The severity of the itch is proportional to the difficulty of
reaching it.

**85**

31.9 per cent of statistics are made up on the spot!

Hard work pays off in the future. Laziness pays off now.

Time is nature's way of keeping everything from happening all at once.

A youthful figure is what you get when you ask a woman her age.

James Thurber wrote, 'I'm 65. I guess that puts me in the geriatrics. But if there were 15 months in the year, I'd only be 48. That is the trouble with us. We number everything. Take women, for example. I think they deserve to have more than 12 years between the ages of 28 and 40!'

One good thing about being bald is that when visitors drop in unexpectedly, all you have to do is straighten your tie.

Why do you have to get old before people say you look young?

NO one is a keener observer of the idiosyncrasies and idiocies of ordinary life than the comedian Billy Connolly. He recalls a lady in Belfast who stopped him in the street and asked, 'Is that you?' When he replied, 'Yes, it's me', she said, 'You know, you look like yourself'. Billy's genius lies in seeing the unexpected humour in 'wellie boots', in getting up in the morning, in commuting, and watching children and grown-ups at play. Who else would have thought to describe Bonnie Prince Charlie as 'the only man to be called after three sheep dogs', or to liken faith to an 'ashtray full of wee doubts'? It is a pity that some of Billy's shows are spoiled by the machine gun fashion in which he sometimes uses the F-word, for the humorous insights of this brilliant comedian of the commonplace do not need that kind of embellishment.

Instead of producing great hilarity, a witticism is apt to produce a mixture of amusement and appreciation coupled with admiration owing to the subtlety. This is the kind of humour I find most appealing, humour which is not only a clever play on the double meanings of words and the queer inconsistencies and oddities of speech, but has truth in it.

✖

Diplomacy is lying in state.

✖

Drive-in banking was invented so that new cars could see their real owners.

✖

What people call congestion in a train is atmosphere in a night-club.

An extravagance is anything you buy that is of no use to your spouse.

A housing development is a place where they cut down all the trees and then name the streets after them.

If you give same people an inch, they quickly think they are rulers.

Inflation is when money still talks, but in an apologetic tone.

A Glasgow journalist pointed out that whereas the tailors in the city used to live above their shops in the Gallowgate, many of them now live above their incomes in suburban Bearsden.

An elderly man surprised his friends by saying, 'Disco music makes me want to clap my hands', but then he added 'over my ears'.

He who laughs last is the one who intended to tell the joke himself.

❋

When at the end of a piano recital by a woman of great technical prowess, Arthur Schnabel was asked what he thought of the performance, he snorted, 'Immaculate, but no conception'.

❋

Life is like a grindstone. Whether it grinds you down or polishes you up depends on what you are made of.

❋

Workmen who were redecorating drab government offices, daubed the words 'Old Macdonald had a Farm' above the sign that indicated rooms 'E1 – E10'.

❋

A reluctant secretary was overheard to say, 'When my husband picked me up and carried me over the threshold, it was not an act of love. He was taking me to work'.

❋

When a woman who had tried on countless pairs of shoes told the assistant that she had to have a pair that were extremely comfortable, for she suffered from water on the knee, the assistant opened another box and said, 'How about *these*. They are pumps'.

Shortly after Churchill was defeated in the General Election at the end of the Second World War, Queen Elizabeth offered to make him a Knight of the Garter – a most illustrious honour. He refused, saying, 'How could I accept the Garter from her majesty when her people have just given me the boot?'

Once at Bournemouth two annual conferences were taking place in neighbouring hotels. One comprised people working in the newspaper business and the other a conference of fish and chip merchants. At its opening session the fish and chip merchants decided to send a telegram of good wishes to the newspaper employees. The telegram read: 'We wish you a successful conference, for, after all, our business is wrapped up in yours.'

Several years ago a magazine ran a poetry contest, setting out three rules for submissions. The poems had to rhyme, be brief, and appeal to most people. The winning poem contained ony two words, PAY/DAY.

That briefest of poems recalled a story of a man carrying a sandwich board on which were written the words, 'The wages of sin is death'. One day he carelessly stepped off the pavement into the path of an on-coming truck. The driver having narrowly missed him, leant out of his window and said, 'What do you think this is – *Pay Day?*'

A man waited wearily while the barber gave the customer before him a summary of the current political situation. At last when his turn came, the barber said, 'And how would you like your hair cut?'

'Preferably in silence!'

Once at a civic dinner I met John, a former university classmate, whom I had not seen for forty years. He had aged so much that he did not recognise me! The following morning as I was shaving, I got to thinking about this. As I looked at my reflection in our new bathroom mirror, it suddenly struck me that they don't make good mirrors any more!

When the actress Sarah Bernhardt was touring the Western States of America, she was interviewed by a reporter for the *Carson Appeal, San Francisco Examiner,* and the Associated Press. Pleased with the way he had handled her story, the emotional actress, as she left, kissed him on both cheeks and then on the lips. 'The kiss on your right cheek is for the *Appeal,* the one on the left is for the *Examiner,* and the one on the lips is for yourself.'

With a mischievous twinkle in his eye, he replied, 'Madame, I also represent the Associated Press which serves *three hundred and eight* newspapers!'

# Puns, Riddles, Wisecracks, Satire

DIFFERENT names have been given to different forms of wit. The **pun**, said Oscar Levant, is the lowest form of humour when you don't think of it first. Some men were pleasantly swapping puns until another joined them. When he wailed disapproval at each new pun, one of the punsters said, 'Stop being a wit blanket'. The comic nature of the pun rests upon its mono-sound and multi-meaning.

�

A good swimmer is one who is *deependable*.

✖

A son writing a long-overdue letter to his parents apologised for his '*unwriteousness*'.

✖

TV and radio presenter Terry Wogan sought to answer a question many have asked: 'Why is it that so many people who live in big houses have receptions in marquees?' Was it, he suggested, because the excitement in a marquee is more *intense*?

✖

Golf-course – a site to be holed.

93

I sometimes wonder if church services during the winter should have a five-minute *coughie* break.

A Sheryl Rogers tells how when a crane one day backed into her path, narrowly missing her car, her companion said, 'That could have been a real crane in the wreck'. The following day, as they passed the same spot, a truck carrying concrete slabs forced them to stop quickly. 'That could have been another crane in the wreck,' she remembered. 'No,' said her friend. 'That would have been a slab in the face.'

A fool and his money are soon *partying*.

Christmas can so easily become a *wrap race*.

It was the first *pair* that ate the first apple.

Too many of us suffer from *I-strain*. Our I's are too close together. When we converse with other egotists, it is an *I for an I*.

The world is a big ball that revolves on its *taxes*.

The man who shops with his wife is usually a *wait-watcher*.

When the bathroom scales are adjusted, you often see the error of your *weighs*.

A refined version of the pun is commonly found in cross-word puzzles:

- What the sailor sits on without results – Hatch.
- The orphan has neither of this, a widely-held view – Panorama.
- Side issue – Eve.
- Children's Nursery – Bawlroom.

Telegrams at weddings often contain puns, none more hackneyed than 'May all your troubles be little ones'. A more original one arrived at a Highland wedding I conducted on the twelfth of August, the traditional date for the start of the grouse-shooting season: 'The dear season is over, the grouse has begun.'

Suggestions why some people retire early:

- Carpet dealer – had made his pile.
- Forester – got the axe.
- Cook – got fed up.
- Vet – got dog-tired.

CLOSELY connected to the pun is the modern version of the **riddle**. A Glasgow riddle posed the question: 'What did they give the person who invented the door-knocker?' Answer: 'The no-bell prize.'

The riddle used to be regarded as the highest form of humour. The most famous of the early riddles was the Sphinx. We still use the phrase, 'You are a perfect sphinx' – meaning that you speak in riddles. The Sphinx was a sea monster that proposed a riddle to the Thebans, and murdered all who could not guess it.

The riddle ran: 'What goes on four feet, on two feet and three, but the more feet it goes on the weaker it be?' When Oedipus finally solved it, the sphinx put herself to death.

The answer was: a human being – first crawling on all fours, then walking upright on two feet, and finally in old age using a staff.

Another famous riddle was that proposed by Samson to the Philistines: 'Out of the eater came forth meat and out of the strong came forth sweetness.'

The answer turned on the young lion that Samson had slain with his own hands, and in whose carcass he later saw a swarm of bees whose honey he extracted.

THE medium of radio elevated the **wisecrack** to its position of pre-eminence in public favour. The need of radio for humorous resources that were not time-consuming, led comedians to opt for the wisecrack and the gag.

Bob Hope is the name most associated with wisecracks. 'There is nothing,' he once said, 'quite like a British summer, except perhaps an Arctic winter.' On another occasion he told of a man who hid his money in the mattress so that he could have something to fall back on.

Training a child is a matter of pot-luck.

A man chases a woman until she catches him.

Child guidance is something parents should provide, not submit to.

Poverty is a wonderful thing. It sticks to a person even when all his friends forsake him.

One reason the average girl would rather have beauty than brains is that she knows the average man can see much better than he can think.

A great thing about children is that they never pull out photographs of their grandparents.

Health warning: 'Gambling is bad for your wealth.'

A hypocrite isn't himself on Sundays.

A good teacher drives you to think.

If you don't want your teenage youngsters to hear what you are saying, pretend you're talking to them.

A Gossip Columnist has a fine sense of rumour.

A director to a lad he was sacking: 'We have done more for you than your mother ever did. We have carried you for 15 months.'

When men argue with their wives, words often flail them.

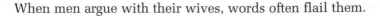

Money doesn't talk any more. It just goes without saying.

You reach a stage when everything clicks – knees, elbows, neck.

A husband told how his wife had undergone plastic surgery. He explained that he had cancelled her credit cards.

The conclusion is the place the author got tired of thinking.

The cock croweth, but the hen delivereth the goods.

When a cynic smells flowers, he looks around for the coffin.

INCLUDED in wit is the whole sphere of **satire**. Satire highlights abuses, follies and idiosyncrasies of all kinds. There was more than a touch of satire in the three examples of oxymorons which Richard Stillgoe gave in a radio broadcast: Military Intelligence, Royal Family and *Sun* Journalist.

A newspaper report told how 'a Help the Poor Committee met for luncheon and resolved to have another luncheon'.

Once a boy carved his name on the old-fashioned desk in the country schoolhouse and grew up without becoming famous.

Faith won't die so long as coloured seed catalogues are printed.

Old age insurance guarantees you steak when your teeth are gone.

Minor operations are those performed on other people.

To err is human, but when the eraser wears out before the pencil, you are overdoing it.

**I**RONY involves saying the opposite of what you mean and the listener believing the opposite of what is said. Irony is present even with children. You see it in the nicknames of our childhood when we called the very tall boy Tiny and the slow boy Speedy. Irony is usually masked in politeness. It is closely related to satire.

---

He was as grateful as an untipped waiter.

---

It was as simple as an Income Tax return.

---

The tired shop attendant had taken down one coloured blanket after another from a high shelf, until only one was left.

Then the customer remarked: 'I don't really want to buy today. I was just looking for a friend.'

'Well,' said the assistant, 'I'll take down the last one if you think your friend might possibly be in it.'

---

A concerned church official was heard to say, 'If absence makes the heart grow fonder, an awful lot of people must love our church.'

AHOOGA!!

# Spoonerisms and Misprints

**SPOONERISMS**, named after the Rev. Dr Spooner of Oxford who was renowned for getting words confused, can be a rich source of amusement.

- The vicar knows every *crook* and *nanny* in this place.
- It is *kist*omary now for the bridegroom to *cuss* the bride.
- It is easier for a camel to go through the *knee* of an *idol* ...
- The next record is for a couple who are celebrating forty years of holy *deadlock.*

We are all at times guilty of such howlers. One man said that his haemorrhoids were a real pain in the *neck*. A friend excused her absence from a meeting by saying that she had been *indecapitated.* A woman was assured by a member of the hospital medical staff that her sister was receiving *RIP* treatment. Another woman was informed she was suffering from *congenial* heart disease. A man lamented to his neighbour that 'a *verbal* contract is not worth the paper it's written on'.

An American who had been delegated to welcome President Herbert Hoover, called him *'Hobart Heever'*. He then corrected it to *'Heeber Hobart'*, before finally saying, 'I give you the President'!

**M**ISPRINTS can also have amusing results. For example, an advert for a Christmas 'Nine Lessons and Carols' service in Winnipeg appeared as 'Wine, Lessons and Carols'. The minister said he had never had such a large congregation!

A choir touring Europe was advertised at one location as being 'internationally renounced'.

A car advert read '1996 Vauxhall Cavalier – floorless condition'.

One student wrote that Louis Pasteur invented a cure for rabbis; another that Socrates died from an overdose of wed-lock.

It was said of one Church Board that there were seven executive staff of whom two were monsters.

A notice on the door of an American restaurant read: 'No bear feet allowed.'

The carpet was treadbare.

Bishop Joe Devine took part in a special TV 'Songs of Praise' service at the time of the Gulf War. That night he was paid a wonderful compliment. One of the hymns appeared in print as 'Love *devine,* all love's excelling'. That reminded me of the couple who asked if they could have at their wedding the romantic hymn, 'Love's divine'.

Before I was installed as Moderator, a former occupant of the chair said to me, 'I will guarantee you one thing. You will grow in stature during your year in office'. I soon discovered what he meant. The tables in church and village halls creaked with 'goodies'. As the year progressed, my wife and I both took comfort from the misprint of a well-known text, 'The earth is the Lord's and all that *swell* therein'.

A highlight of my moderatorial visit to Malawi was meeting with Liz Mantell, one of our medical missionaries. Liz had been for many years an outstanding sister tutor of trainee midwives. She enjoyed sharing with me a letter she had received from a Malawi girl. It began 'Dear Sister *Mental,* I would like to train to be a *mad*wife ....'

Nancy Dimmock tells of a new missionary in Africa who was struggling with the native language. She began her talk to a group of women with what she thought was 'My life is divided into two parts'. This was greeted with loud laughter, for what she had said was 'My rear end is divided into two parts'.

The Rev. Margaret Forrester tells how she attended one of the early services of ordination for woman priests in the Anglican Church. Outside the church that day were several women protesting against the ordination of women. In the Order of Service were the words of a new hymn, a hymn based on Jesus stilling the storm on the Lake of Galilee. The opening line should have read, 'Rage, rage, ye waves', but read instead, 'Rage, rage, ye *wives*'.

Jordanhill Church in Glasgow received an invoice from James Ferguson Decorators, Milngavie, for external painter-work to the manse. A typing error resulted in the invoice being headed '*eternal* painterwork'. I am sure many church treasurers wished all painters gave such 'lasting' guarantees.

Peter Ustinov tells how, as a small boy, he was terrified when his mother one Christmas told him she was going to take him to Harrod's. When they got near the door of the famous London department store, he turned and ran. Recalling what King Herod had done to little boys, there was no way he was going anywhere near *Herod's*.

The notice in the church bulletin should have read, 'This Thursday the Ladies Group will meet for the second in a series of "Studies in the Bible"', but in fact it read '*Studs* in the Bible'.

A minister tells how, one autumn, in his church newsletter, he expressed the hope that for every organisation it would be a successful winter session, that all their plans would duly come to fruition. But the printer's proof, when it arrived, expressed the hope that all their plans would duly come to *friction.*

Well aware of the tensions that existed within the congregation, tensions between the Boys Brigade and the Badminton Club, tensions within the choir, and in the Session, between the liberal and more conservative elders, the minister was glad he had spotted the misprint at the proof stage.

An American congregation, divided over whether to use debts or trespasses in the Lord's Prayer, finally decided to use a different version: 'Forgive us our sins as we forgive those who sin against us.' They also agreed that, for the first few weeks, the new text would appear in the printed Order of Service. Unfortunately, due to a typing error, it appeared as – 'as we forgive those who *win* against us'.

At the end of the service the church baseball coach suggested to the minister that this version would be appropriate for their struggling team!

Dr Roy Sanderson tells how a letter arrived one day at the church offices addressed not to the Right Rev. Dr Sanderson, but 'the *Tight* Rev.'!

The following notice appeared in the handbook for patients in a Leominster Hospital: 'Clergy of all dimensions are welcome to visit the hospital.'

# Clangers

UNINTENTIONAL humour is very common. How often we say things which later we wish we had not said. At other times we embarrass ourselves by speaking before we think.

ON a visit to England, an American tourist and his wife came one lunchtime to a place where bands were playing and flags flying. Inquiring about the excitement, he was told the people were celebrating the anniversary of the signing of the Magna Charta at Runnymede.

'When did it take place?' he asked.

When the local resident replied '1215', the American looked at his watch and said, 'Sorry honey, we've missed it by fifteen minutes'.

The following notice appeared in a church newsletter: 'Weight watchers will meet at 6.30 pm. Please use the large double door on the North side.'

The note of appreciation for a new loud speaking system could have been better worded: 'The loud speakers in the church are being given by one of our members in memory of his wife.'

A grandmother told me how, when her grand-daughter visits, she loves to slip into bed with her. Early one morning as she snuggled in, she said, 'Grandma you look more beautiful in the dark'.

In Peterhead, at the turn of the century, Baillie Duncan's wife gave birth to their twenty-fourth child. Like the previous twenty-three, the latest was born at home. As the doctor completed the form to be taken to the registrar, he turned to Baillie Duncan. Inquiring about the date, he asked, 'Is this the *26th?*' Thinking the doctor was inquiring about the size of his family, the father replied, 'Oh no doctor. It's *just* the twenty-fourth'.

The film star Kirk Douglas in his autobiography tells how he once stopped to pick up a young soldier who was thumbing a lift. Shortly after the young man got in the car, he turned and looked at Kirk Douglas. There then followed a double-take, resulting in the soldier blurting out, 'Do you know who you are?'

A lady in New York, who had looked very closely at the elderly James Mason, finally approached him and said, 'Are you James Mason in his later years?'

A minister who had been given a twenty-fifth anniversary holiday by his congregation, said at the close of his last service before setting out, 'God be with you until I return'. Not surprisingly he later shuddered at the implications of what he had said.

Considerable confusion can be caused by church ministers wearing mufti instead of clerical attire.

At a dinner at which I was to speak, I was introduced to another top-table guest. Forgetting that I was wearing dinner suit and bow-tie, I said, 'We actually met a few years ago. I married your niece Nancy Haddow'.

With a look of disbelief on his face, he said, 'But Ian Rule married Nancy'.

Then I had to explain that what I meant was I had officiated at their wedding.

A woman minister tells of causing even greater confusion. She was once rushing from a meeting to conduct a service at the crematorium. On the way she was flagged down by a lady driver who was lost. Remembering the story of the good Samaritan, she stopped and gave directions. The lady not only thanked her, but started to tell her life-story.

As they were conversing a hearse went by. The woman minister, forgetting she was not wearing any distinctive clerical clothing, said, 'I am sorry, I will have to go. That is my funeral and I must get to the crematorium before the coffin'. The lady driver visibly paled.

Shortly after landing in Manila in the Philippines to preside at the Johnnie Walker Golf Classic, Lord Macfarlane said, 'I would like to thank the Philistines ... er, Filipinos ... for their warm welcome'. Beware of jet lag!

[Why is it that the word Philippines is spelt with 'Ph' and a double 'p', and 'Filipinos with an 'F' and one 'p'?]

At a dance one night a man approached the band and asked if they played requests. When the bandmaster asked what piece of music he wanted, he replied, 'Anything'.

The Rev. J McGhie tells of visiting an elderly lady. As they chatted she said, 'What I like about you is that I can talk to you as if you were a man'.

A girl wrote to a magazine agony aunt, explaining that she had been courting this boy for a month. 'I now discover he has a wooden leg. Should I break it off?'

A Canadian boys club decided to try to break the world record for non-stop see-sawing. Shortly before they were due to reach the formidable target of over 250 hours, they learned that it was in fact over 300 hours. They decided to press on and make a new record. When the grandmother of one of the boys heard of what had happened, she said she was very glad the boys had found out in time; otherwise it would have been an awful waste of time!

The office lay-about was staring out of the window. When asked what intrigued him, he said, 'I have been watching that road-worker for twenty minutes and he has not done a stroke'.

When Dr James Weatherhead went to be measured for a new suit, the usual measurements were taken. He was told to stretch out his arm and then bend it. He was however slightly puzzled when at one stage the tailor asked him to raise his right foot. Never having been asked to do this before, he enquired why.

'Because,' said the tailor, 'you are standing on my tape.'

An old man who was dying asked his wife if she might be willing to sit beside his sister at his funeral. His wife, who could not stand her sister-in-law, grudgingly agreed.

'But I hope you realise,' she added, 'that it will completely spoil my day.'

At the time when his popular Sunday evening television lectures were being screened by the BBC, Professor William Barclay was on holiday in Troon. He later enjoyed recounting how, during breakfast on the Monday morning, an American lady kept glancing over to his table. Finally she came over and said, 'Are you the Dr Barclay who was on television last night?'

When he told her he was, she said, 'Do you have a church?'

'No,' he said, intending to go on and explain that he taught New Testament to student ministers.

But before he could do so, she put her hand on his shoulder and said, 'Don't worry. I think you will get one soon'.

Each year the Moderator of the General Assembly of the Church of Scotland is invited to preach for the Royal Family at Crathie Church and to spend the weekend at Balmoral Castle. A former Moderator was so afraid that at some time during his year in office he might lose the historic Moderatorial ring, that he arranged for a duplicate to be made. At the dinner table he not only told her Majesty of his fear, but then added, 'The ring I am in fact wearing tonight is the duplicate. I keep the original for special occasions'.

Marj Carpenter tells of a minister and his family who were stopped by a police car. When the policeman asked the minister how fast he thought he was travelling, he replied, 'I admit I was driving about five miles an hour above the speed limit. You're not going to give me a ticket for that, are you?'

When the policeman said that this time he would only give him a warning, the minister's six year old son piped up from the back of the car, 'That's what that other policeman said last week'.

An Arran McKee tells how, after visiting a young business client, she typed a letter of thanks. The word processor's spelling check having indicated no errors, she posted the letter. The next meeting was so frosty that she re-read her original letter. To her dismay she discovered that it read: 'Thank you for your time toady … I look forward to seeing you again son.'

A bride travelling with her father to the church in a white Rolls Royce, bedecked with white ribbons, was stopped by a young road census official, armed with a clip-board. He solemnly enquired, 'Could you tell me the purpose of your journey?'

## Previous Publications by
## The Rev James A Simpson

*Doubts are not enough* (Saint Andrew Press: Edinburgh).

*Keywords of Faith* (Saint Andrew Press: Edinburgh).

*There is a Time to ...* (James Clark & Co Ltd: Cambridge).

*The Master Mind* (Handsel Press Ltd: Musselburgh).

*Holy Wit* (Gordon Wright Publishing Ltd: Edinburgh).

*More Holy Wit* (Gordon Wright Publishing Ltd: Edinburgh).

*Laughter Lines* (Gordon Wright Publishing Ltd: Edinburgh).

*All about Christmas: The Traditions and Meaning of the Festive Season ...* (Gordon Wright Publishing: Edinburgh).